HEALING YOUR HEARTBREAK

28 Days to Transformation

Shelley J Whitehead

BALBOA.PRESS

A DIVISION OF HAY HOUSE

Balboa Press books may be ordered through booksellers or by contacting:

Balboa Press
A Division of Hay House
1663 Liberty Drive
Bloomington, IN 47403
www.balboapress.co.uk
UK TFN: 0800 0148647 (Toll Free inside the UK)
UK Local: (02) 0369 56325 (+44 20 3695 6325 from outside the UK)

Illustrations by Kerry Lea Peterkin.
Book design by LIVE Creative (www.livecreative.co.za).
Author photograph by Nic Voutsas.

Print information available on the last page.

ISBN: 978-1-9822-8780-1 (sc)
ISBN: 978-1-9822-8781-8 (hc)
ISBN: 978-1-9822-8779-5 (e)

Library of Congress Control Number: 2024901067

Balboa Press rev. date: 01/30/2024

*I lovingly dedicate this book
to my dear Aunt Vonnie, who
taught me to shine.*

Table of contents

Prologue

In the grips of heartbreak, your world might be feeling utterly desolate and barren. If you are clinging on to the hope that the relationship hasn't really ended, the sense of disorientation can make you dizzy. You may feel stiff with fear. Your inner voice may be silenced, trapped within the agonising feeling of loss. And your sense of worth might be rock-bottom.

It's soul-rupturing. I've been there. I know the pain, oh-so-well.

You are in the right place, my lovely! I'm going to guide you out of this sense of devastation, through healing and into strength.

But this book isn't just about 'recovery'. I don't want to just get you back to the place you were before. It is about the transformative power of rupture. You see, the thing I learnt about heartbreak - from my own personal journey into the murkiest depths of despair - was that, if you allow it, your experience will open up the way for a kind of liquid gold to seep into the cracks of your broken heart. That gold will fuse into your being, to make you and your life more magical, more soulful and more beautiful than you could ever have imagined.

If you can go with the flow a little, this pain that has stopped you in your tracks will take you to the depths of your soul, where you will almost touch a divine sense of your place in the great swirling movement of the universe. Rather than pure devastation, it can be a profound and life-affirming experience. A fresh wave of your story. You will never be the same again - you will be more grounded, vibrant and powerful than you have ever felt before.

All of this might be impossible to imagine right now. The way out of this pain might feel like an insurmountable mountain to climb and far too much effort! That's where I come in. I'll be with you, every step of the way. 28 steps in total. One step at a time. Let's do this, together!

The healing mindset

Let's get you in the right mindset for your healing journey. There are a few things I'd like you to keep in mind as you work through this book …

Healing requires a balance of focus and kindness

You will find that you reap the greatest benefits if you do the exercises in sequence, step by step, and ensure that you have completed each one before you move onto the next. As you work your way through, you will find that you are not only healing but that you are becoming an ever-increasingly radiant version of yourself. In order to keep your momentum going, my recommendation is that you make a commitment to complete the whole book within a specific time frame. If you can keep to the rhythm you have defined for yourself, you will find that momentum builds and has a beautiful snowball-like effect, with your healing naturally accelerating as you get further through the process. But you need to work at a pace that works for YOU and allows you flexibility. If you want to do this in 28 days consecutively that's great … if you decide to work through the 28 steps over three months, that's fine too. Remember: always be kind to yourself! Take your time.

Healing is an active process

It's really important to actually take the steps, rather than just *thinking* about taking the steps. True healing comes from embodied and committed action. It is hard to sustain real change if you have only thought about changing. All of the steps are carefully crafted and curated to help you weave profound change into your spirit, but they will only work their magic if you give yourself the gift of committing to fully doing the work. All of the steps are designed to be bite-sized and manageable because grief requires structure and slowness. You will find that the more steps you do the more pleasurable the process becomes. Before long, you will start to really enjoy yourself!

Healing is an 'iterative' journey

Change is not a one-stop shop! This book is designed as the beginning of a journey. It will change the course of your life and turn your trajectory around, from a place of pain and despair into a journey of wildly beautiful discovery. So don't be surprised if there are steps within this that you feel you would like to explore more. Think of this book as a helicopter view on a foundation course of healing. As you work through the book, note down the areas you would like to commit to exploring more and circle back to in the future.

Healing is an act of courage

With me as your guide, you can do this. Even if you feel as though you are in the depths of darkness and even if you can't see it right now, there is a glimmer of light for you, on the horizon. Allow my words to enfold you and to soothe you as I take you by the hand and guide you forwards. This is how you start to build a new story and rediscover your courage and your smile. Oh yes you will! There is hope. By picking up this book, you have already started your healing journey. Have courage! There's light ahead.

*Awakening is not a process
of building ourselves up but
a process of letting go.*

- Pema Chödrön

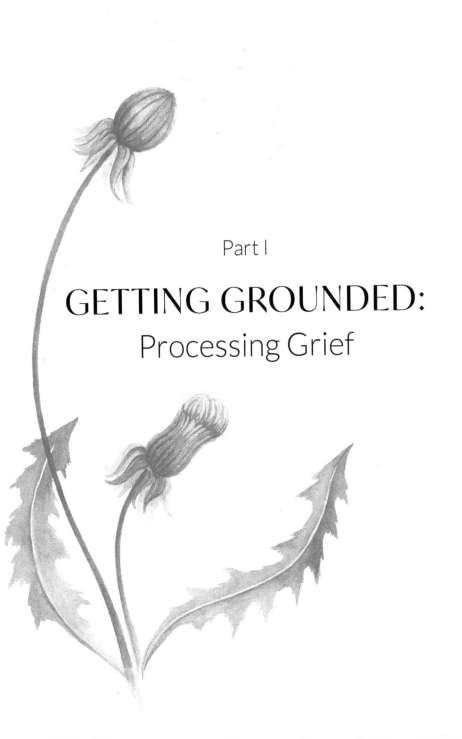

Part I

GETTING GROUNDED:
Processing Grief

Have you ever had one of those moments in life when you feel as though you are having an out-of-body experience? When you suddenly feel as though you are looking through the threads of the fabric of the universe and you suddenly understand the pattern that cloth is woven in?

That was me. On my knees in my garden, some fifteen years ago. In the deathly grips of the most agonising pain I had ever experienced: the intense pain of heartbreak.

At that point in my life, heartbreak wasn't an unfamiliar sensation to me. I had been there, again and again, from my earliest days of dating. But this time it was different. This time, the heartbreak was accompanied by the deepest of betrayals. My partner of seven years - my best friend - had betrayed me and then, unceremoniously and seemingly out of nowhere, dumped me. As though the past had never existed and as though I had never meant anything to him, I found myself cast aside. Dismissed. Without a hint of regret or anguish on his part, he'd left me for someone else.

I was humiliated, hurt, angry, confused, frustrated, sad, lonely ... the list went on. I was completely lost in a sea of the most horrifically painful and disorienting of emotions.

My usual response to that level of pain was to flee from it, in whatever way possible. My default coping mechanism was to distract myself. I would lose myself in work, throw myself into running after my children, get busy with tidying the house, and spend hours talking round and round in circles with my friends ... anything to keep me out of the agonising feeling of sinking into pain. That was exactly what I had been doing for months, going through the motions and showing up as

2

a ghostly shell in my daily life, desperately and frantically trying to stay busily distracted. Even the smallest of tasks felt impossible and monumental, but I needed to keep busy with them, all the time.

And here I was in my garden, on my knees pruning a rose, doing exactly that - keeping busy to numb the feelings.

But something stopped me in my tracks.

As I vigorously chopped away at the thorny stems, I felt the tears welling up inside me. I tried, as usual, to choke them back, chopping faster and faster as the poor innocent rose was being whittled away to almost nothing.

I looked around me. The bleak winter garden was in a dormant state. Most of the plants were tightly hunkered down. The trees were naked, having shed their autumn leaves, in their annual dormant slumber. Everything around me was still and quiet. What on earth was I doing pruning a rose bush in the depths of winter?

Suddenly the tears started to sputter out of me like an unstoppable river and a voice in my head said to me: 'This is grief. Let it flow.'

Let it flow.

Of course. I was grieving. Why had I never associated heartbreak with grief before? It was so obvious. As a trained grief coach, I had spent many years holding the space for my clients, encouraging them to surrender to the magical process of grief. And yet, somehow, I had never connected the dots.

Just as my garden had quietened into its wintery state, I needed to allow myself to go into my own kind of dormancy for a while, through the container of grief. I needed to let go and allow myself to go fully into my own winter of grief and to no longer use the shield of busyness to try to outrun the feelings. It was time to be still.

My acceptance of my own grief was the beginning of my personal journey into becoming the person I am today. A person who is more whole, more grounded and more alive than I had ever been up to that point. The journey was so powerfully transformative that it is now at the heart of my professional world too. It's something I take profound joy in sharing, as I have seen how it can change lives in the most wonderful way. More on that later.

For now, I want you to have courage in taking the first step of this journey with me.

1.

Going with the
flow of grief

The first thing we're going to do is to get you grounded in some clarity. Through that clarity you will start to see some of the first little chinks of sunlight through the dark storm of confusion, pain and anguish. The starting point is knowing that grief itself is not just natural - it is an important and powerfully regenerative process.

You're not crazy - you are grieving

When I made a personal connection between grieving and heartbreak, I felt a deep sense of relief that I wasn't going crazy. The swirling mix of emotions I was going through was totally understandable.

This is what I'd like you to recognise for yourself now: if you are going through heartbreak, you are grieving.

Heartbreak is a form of grief. It might not be a physical death that you are grieving, but a metaphorical death (of a relationship or of the vision you had of your future) can be just as painful. Grief is one of the most intense experiences you can go through, because it is a close partner of love: if you are experiencing grief, it means that you have loved.

When you have lost someone through a physical death, society has a place for your pain, usually embodied in a set of rituals to help you through. When you're in the early stages of shock after someone has died, people might bring round food or send cards of condolence, to let you know they are there for you and thinking about you. A funeral is then a moment that people come together to celebrate the life that once was and to mark and honour the ending. In social terms, it's acceptable to cry and acceptable to not be at your best. In essence, you are given space and support for your grief.

When a relationship ends, however, society can become a little awkward around the subject. In the early stages of my own heartbreak grief, I was told repeatedly to just get over it and move on. It was said in a well-meaning way, but it wasn't helpful. I needed to make sense of what had happened.

This kind of 'disenfranchisement' (in other words, something people pretend doesn't exist) can push you into a form of self-denial, where you either rush through your healing or try to deny the validity of your pain altogether.

There is no rushing or denying grief.

When you can connect with your grief, you can allow the wisdom of the viscerally felt experience of your emotions to work their magic whilst you digest the magnitude and the meaning of the shock and the loss.

Grieving is restorative

We live in a culture obsessed with continual growth. A culture that encourages us to learn, to strive, to push and to shift ahead relentlessly. Growth at any cost. And often that cost is high because, without rest, growth can turn into overload.

There are times when we need to pull back and pause. Times when we need to allow the natural self-healing properties of the body and mind to knit strength back into our beings and ready us for what lies ahead. The seasons cycle and there is a time and a place for everything. In the wintry state of grief, you can allow yourself to focus all of your energy on just putting one foot in front of the other.

If you surrender to grief, you won't drown. Quite the opposite! It is a healing process. Resist the flow of the grief and you might find that you become frozen in time and unable to move on. But if you immerse yourself in it, your grief will carry you through a readjustment period, whilst you reset into a new reality. The new reality without the person you loved by your side. Ultimately, you will come to see it as a better reality. You will survive the loss and will emerge, phoenix-like, with a renewed sense of self and sense of your future.

Grief flows through six stages

I'm going to introduce you to the 'six stages' of grief, so you can start to relax into that flow a little. As you're reading your way through this, you may have a few 'aha' moments, where you recognise some of the experiences you have been going through.

The six-stage model (defined by the brilliant psychologist Elisabeth Kübler-Ross) describes the series of emotive spaces that people typically go through when they are grieving. On the basis of my personal epiphany about heartbreak being closely related to grief, I adapted this model and found that I could apply the same understanding to support people who were recovering from a broken heart.

Stage 1 - Denial

The first stage of grieving is denial. If your partner ended the relationship, the feelings of rejection and abandonment can be sky high. In the midst of the hurt and humiliation, you might be feeling hopeful that your ex finds the world unbearable without you and comes back - and in doing this, you receive a temporary relief from the pain. Denial is a readily understandable natural first response to heartbreak and is the mind's way of helping you to allow a bit of information in at a time, so you don't slip into overwhelm. Like any system, trying to take on too much at once can cause a kind of mental short circuiting - the fuse trips and we shut down. When we go into overwhelm, an experience can be registered as a 'trauma', which means that healing can be impaired. So, the natural process of dipping in and out of denial is a helpful way for the mind to dip its toe in and out of reality, gradually adjusting to the road ahead.

Stage 2 - Anger

After the initial shock of a breakup wears off and reality starts to sink in, big emotions can take over – and anger can be the biggest of them all. If your partner lied, was abusive or left you for someone else, you may feel more distraught than you've felt in any previous breakup. The interesting thing about anger is that it tells us about who we are as a person, as it helps us to define and clarify our boundaries (with boundaries being defined as the difference between 'where I start and end' and 'where you start and end' - myself as an independent entity). So the value of anger in the grieving process is that it allows us to start to redefine the future as full and independent entities (the 'who I am without you').

Stage 3 - Bargaining

This is similar to the first stage in that it involves a degree of denial. It's a softer form of denial though, where we can admit to ourselves that the relationship has ended, but we hold onto the hope that we may still get them back. After a breakup, you might find yourself thinking 'if only I can find the right thing to say to them, they'll come back to me' ... and similar things that allow you to hold onto the fantasy that you might still get them back. It's quite common to cycle through the first three stages in an obsessive loop as you try to work out 'what went wrong'. It's also quite common for people to try to reignite a relationship with the bargaining plea of 'I promise I will change'. This is particularly the case for those who have been 'dumped' (oh how I HATE that word 'dumped', but it is so expressive and apt for those of us who have ever been carelessly and heartlessly dismissed by someone!). Bargaining is all part of the readjustment and slow adaptation to the new reality. It's a step forward from the stage of denial, yet still a place of hovering between the new reality and the past.

Stage 4 - Depression

As you process the hurt and disappointment at the loss of future dreams and start to let go of the denial and bargaining, this initial shock and anger can give way to a sense of depression. As you emerge from the obsessive loop of the first three stages, you might be faced with the weight and heaviness of the realisation that nothing you can do will change things, causing depression to set in. Allowing yourself to feel this heavy emotion isn't a bad thing and is, in fact, an important part of healing. It's better not to deny your feelings but to allow them in, acknowledge them and honour them. When you hit the point of depression, it's like hitting the bottom on a deep dive. That's it – there's no more denying the pain, the loss, the heartbreak. Once you have allowed yourself to fully experience that pain you will find that you start to become ready to accept it.

Stage 5 - Acceptance

Acceptance is the moment at which you find yourself able to let go of the fantasy and the loss, move on from the anger and emerge like a phoenix from the depression. My process, contained in the pages of this book, will be a wonderful catalyst and guiding force to help you to get there ... and go far beyond.

Stage 6 - Finding Meaning

In our journey together in this book you'll find your way through acceptance and into the place where you can start to find meaning. Your life ahead will be all the stronger for the journey you have been through, and these healing tools will help you to transform your life in ways you would not have dreamed possible.

A journey through grief isn't linear. You might feel like you're going round in circles through the stages - that's all totally normal. Remember: it won't last forever.

Today you're going to ... understand your grieving process

We've just skimmed over the six stages of grief. I'd like you to think about how you are feeling right now, in your heartbroken state, and complete the sentences below. Make sure you write them out rather than just think about them. This is just an exercise in observation, so it's important that you don't just think. And don't judge any feelings that come up as you write. By completing these sentences, you will start to have a little bit of understanding about where you are on your journey through grief.

I can't believe that ....

....

....

....

....

....

....

I am angry that ....

....

....

....

....

....

....

If only . . . .
. . . .
. . . .
. . . .
. . . .
. . . .
. . . .

In this depressed state I feel . . . .
. . . .
. . . .
. . . .
. . . .
. . . .

I accept that . . . .
. . . .
. . . .
. . . .
. . . .
. . . .
. . . .

The part that makes sense to me is . . . .
. . . .
. . . .
. . . .
. . . .
. . . .

2.

Getting through denial

Before I had my little 'epiphany' in my garden, I just couldn't quite accept that my relationship had ended. I was holding onto the idea that the relationship was still there and that we might get back together again.

In the very early stages of grieving, denial can be very helpful, as it allows us a bit of mental 'breathing space' to adjust to our new reality. But this early stage of grief is actually one that I often see people getting stuck in and unable to move out of.

I'm going to explain why this can happen and give you a wonderful exercise that will help you to get unstuck.

Tunnel vision keeps you in denial

When my husband first left, I spent several months fixated on the idea that he would come to his senses. Even when I found out I had been 'replaced', it still took me some time to let go.

When you have lost a relationship, it can feel impossible to focus on anything else. This is often because the brain can't take in the fact that the relationship is over, so it can get 'fixated' on holding onto it.

The experience of heartbreak is also the experience of loss. If something is lost, your brain locks into 'search and seek' mode. When you lose your keys, for example, your brain narrows its focus into a kind of 'tunnel vision' - all you can think about is finding the keys. This limited frame of reference isn't helpful. Your diverted energy means you can't see what else is possible or achievable - you are unable to create more resourceful perceptions and responses.

Opening your awareness helps you get through denial

It is really important that you 'open your awareness', to allow for the possibility of a broader perspective. When you do this, you will find that you naturally start to become more resourceful. The fact that you have found your way to this book in the first place means that you are already in a place of accessing resources. So, give yourself a loving pat on the back for that one! That's a good first step in opening up your awareness to other possibilities. If, however, you are finding that ALL you can think about is your ex and that you don't feel in any way ready to even start to consider the possibility of moving on, you may find that you can gain a real sense of relief by doing an exercise that gets you thinking in a more 'open' way about the possibility that lies ahead of you.

Today you're going to ... see some benefits

I'd like you to take a moment to write out a list of all the positive things you can think of that NOT being with your ex now brings you.

This exercise is all about stimulating your imagination and, in doing this, opening up your mind a little. This focus on the future will be a small step away from fixating on the past. Remember that all of these exercises are a series of tiny steps that will take you, one by one, towards a new path ahead. Trust me when I say that even if you can't see the benefit right now, over time it will all start to make sense.

People react in different ways to this exercise. Some find that 25 can be a stretch whilst others make it all the way up to 100 and could go beyond. I encourage you to keep going and to dig deep. Personally, I found 53! In the most unhinged and darkest days of my heartbreak experience, I created this exercise for myself and found that it was very powerful in shifting my perspective out of denial and into focusing my energy in a different direction to the past.

The important thing about this exercise is that you keep going until you get to at least 25. The reason for this is that it forces you to really dig into the unconscious recesses of your mind. This active process of looking for benefits opens your mind up to other possibilities ... and helps you gain momentum with your healing process.

The 25 benefits of not being with my ex are ...

1. ....
   ....

2. ....
   ....

3. ....
   ....

4. ....
   ....

5. ....
   ....

6. ....
   ....

7. ....
   ....

8. ....
   ....

9. ....
   ....

10. ....
    ....

11. ....
    ....

12. ....
    ....

13. ....
    ....

14. ....
....
15. ....
....
16. ....
....
17. ....
....
18. ....
....
19. ....
....
20. ....
....
21. ....
....
22. ....
....
23. ....
....
24. ....
....
25. ....
....

3.

Acknowledging anger

In this next step, we're going to focus on expressing anger. You may already be doing a lot of that already. Or you may be in complete denial about your anger. Either way—or if you are somewhere in between—continue to 'go with the flow' with me on this one. The more you stay on the path of this journey, the more you will start to see how the threads are weaving together, to knit you back into a place of wholeness.

The value of anger

As children we are often taught to reject and repress certain emotions – anger being a really good example. However, like all emotions, anger is important and gives us access to powerful information about ourselves and our relationship with the world. Critically, it allows us to define our boundaries. It tells us where boundaries are being crossed and where we need to do work to protect or assert a boundary. It has a central place in our lives in keeping us tuned into what is important to us and, as a result, understanding who we are.

In not being allowed to express any form of anger when I was growing up, I entered adulthood as an anger-impaired individual, which meant that I bottled it up inside me until it would occasionally 'leak' out in an unconscious or unleashed way. I could either be too submissive or fiery! Neither were conducive to healthy partnership-minded relationships! It took me years of repair work to find my natural sense of self and channel my emotions into an appropriate and balanced sense of self and self-protection. The first step towards that was learning to acknowledge it and express it.

Why it's important to acknowledge emotions

Quite simply, an emotion is a sensation in the body. Therapists and coaches often refer to this as a 'somatic sensation', meaning that it is something that occurs in the body rather than in the mind. Emotions are experienced in the body; thoughts are experienced in the mind.

I think that the best way to understand the meaning and therefore the value of emotions is to see them as 'messengers', interpreting and connecting us to the world around us and framing our experiences. In the same way that we have sensations, such as hunger and thirst, connecting us to our interior landscape and what we need to do to keep it in balance and good health, our emotions connect us to our external landscape.

Today you're going to ... allow yourself to feel the anger

For this exercise, I'd like you to think of all the ways in which you are feeling angry about the breakup and put down the words representing those feelings within the outline below. Swear words are allowed! As you are writing down the words, allow yourself to feel those sensations in your body.

What you do next is then up to you. Some people like to cut around the outline, tape it to a cushion and give it a bit of a beating! Others like to cut it out and then chop it up into tiny little pieces! And some like to take a match to the foot of the page and watch it burn. Let loose! The important thing is that you feel the feelings a little, even if only for a brief moment in time.

4.

Breaking free from bargaining

Bargaining with the past is a horrible thing to get stuck in. In the early days of my heartbreak, I went round and round in circles with the 'if onlys'. It was only when I took the coaching toolkit I had used with my clients and started applying it to break my own obsessive loops, that I started to feel a bit of a sense of relief and my perspective started to come back. I'm going to give you a bit of background about why these loops can be so tricky to overcome and then share an incredibly helpful tool with you.

It's hard to let go because love can be addictive

If your heartbreak relates to splitting up with someone in the early stages of a relationship, there is something very particular that will be happening in your body and brain.

When we fall in love, the brain releases lots of 'feel good' chemicals, associated with pleasure and reward (dopamine) and mood regulation and happiness (serotonin). The increased physical connection we enjoy in a relationship sparks neurotransmitters, which bond us to the other person (oxytocin). This delicious cocktail of chemicals has highly addictive qualities. When anthropologist Dr Helen Fisher carried out MRI scans on people in love, she found activity in the same area of the brain that reacts when people get a cocaine rush. Her conclusion was that romantic love is not an emotion. Rather, it's a drive coming from the brain's 'motor', the part of the brain associated with motivation, focus, craving and obsession. She described love as feeling like 'someone camping in your head'. Sound familiar?

Rejection makes this obsessive craving worse. When a relationship ends, the drop in supply of these neurotransmitters causes withdrawal similar to that of an addict quitting a substance.

No wonder we feel so awful when we can't have who we want! This deficit makes us feel alone, anxious and desperate to connect with our ex. Which is why we might start behaving rashly and in ways that we don't recognise ourselves.

Repetitive thinking is normal. Repetitive thinking is normal.

In heartbreak, not only have you lost something that your body is craving, you are also often desperate to find a reason for *why* it has been lost, even if it was you who instigated the ending. Even if someone has given you a reason for the ending of this relationship or even if you think you have a clear reason yourself, it is hard to let go of the questions around 'why did this happen?'

That's because our brains are hardwired to seek patterns and to understand things, particularly in the case of pain and pain avoidance. Our brain tries to put the pieces of the puzzle together, to avoid having to experience that pain ever again.

It's part of human psychology that we are driven by the desire to minimise loss. Our brains have evolved to hold onto things that feel of value and significance to us. Loss is a form of change and dealing with change takes a tremendous amount of energy, so our instincts lead us to want to avoid change and therefore avoid loss.

We can get stuck asking ourselves 'why did this happen?' The answers to that question just aren't that simple. Sometimes things don't work out. Sometimes people fall out of love or want different things. It feels unfair and it's so painful to accept. You will come out of the other side of this, but staying in this rut won't help you get the answers. (We'll get you there in a much more powerful and productive way, through this journey we're on together in this book.)

I remember myself being in this stage of crazy thinking, unable to focus. I would go down endless rabbit holes of trying to work it all out, occasionally surfacing an intense irritation with myself, 'come ON Shelley!' until I reminded myself that I had the keys to process things. Even with my own specialised knowledge and personal insight, I still had to remind myself of that at least 77 times a day. But mastering my thoughts marked the beginning of channelling my energy back into creating a new life.

Everything you're feeling is normal. It's normal to feel grief when a relationship ends. It's normal to think about the same things over and over again. But obsessing over your ex only prolongs the pain. By letting your ex live on in your thoughts, you are continuing to share your daily life with them. You aren't sharing your life with a real version of them though, you are sharing your life with the ghost of them. When a relationship is over, it's time to let them out of your life. It's time to—FIRMLY—blast away those obsessive thoughts!

I call those obsessive thoughts 'thought monsters' ...

Today you're going to ... stop obsessing

This is a visualisation exercise that will help you if you have the feeling that you're going round and round in circles. If you practise this exercise repeatedly, you will find that the obsessive loops will start to ease off a little. You can repeat this exercise as often as you like. Whenever you start to feel obsessive, you've allowed your thought monsters to multiply. It takes practice and you may see reminders of your ex everywhere, but YOU can switch off the thinking – just like that!

Make sure you're sitting comfortably.

Imagine your obsessive thoughts about your ex have a shape ... any shape.

There's no right or wrong shape to choose – just a shape you want.

Other thoughts will come to distract you. Just push them out of the way and stick to the process.

Now give this shape a colour ... any colour. Perfect.

OK, now start to picture the shape of a body with arms, legs and a little face. This is a 'thought monster'! You can even give these thought monsters a name. I called mine 'Despairing Denise' and 'Anxsty Annie'!

Now imagine that on the right-hand side of your head—next to your right eye—there's a little gold door.

Open it and see all these obsessive little thought monsters cowering in the corner.

Thank them for the work they are doing for you—for the protection they are trying to bring you in hanging around—and then tell them that you are now going to focus on more productive things. Tell them that it's time for you to say goodbye to them and time for you to heal.

Now you have a choice!

Imagine yourself using a hose to dissolve them. A fire hose to turn them into little piles of dust, or a water hose to create little puddles. Obliterate them now! GOOD.

Now take a tiny vacuum cleaner to clear this space and picture it sparkling with bright white light.

Notice how pristine this space is now. Clear. Energised.

Close the door and open your eyes.

5.

Supporting yourself through depression

Remember I told you about that moment when I was on my knees in my garden and the tears started fully flowing? That was the moment when I allowed myself to sink into the depths of the feelings of depression. What I now know is that I needed to surrender to the painfulness of those sensations and hit my 'rock bottom' in order to start to rise back up to the surface again. Like anger, depression is an important emotion that you shouldn't resist when you are grieving. Depression will help you let go and surrender to the things that aren't serving you.

So this step is not about resisting depression. It is about supporting yourself when you are in this place. It's not a comfortable place to be but if you can let the feelings flow, you will find that they start to carry away some of your pain.

Why the tears?

Is it normal to cry bucketloads? Yes, oh yes. Clients often tell me that friends have suggested they need antidepressants to stop this crying. That's often because the *friends themselves* can't cope with seeing their obvious distress.

But you don't need to suppress your feelings. While medication is helpful and necessary at times, crying is a normal response when something makes us very sad. In fact, science has revealed how tears are actually physiologically helpful.

If (like me) you're someone who likes a concrete scientific explanation, here's something you might find interesting: a Yale University study revealed how crying can help us to restore emotional balance. That's because when we're crying we breathe more quickly, taking in much-needed air, which regulates and calms the brain and body. Most importantly, crying activates the parasympathetic nervous system and releases two feel-good chemicals to help ease distress: oxytocin (that same chemical that we feel in the early stages of love, which boosts feelings of connection and can give you a sense of 'calm after the storm') and endorphins (which are released after exercise and can make you feel zoned out or numb, easing the pain).

So, consider crying a helpful way to self-soothe. Don't be afraid of your tears. Sadness and depression are an important part of grieving. Right now, you need rest from the pain of loss and crying can be your emotional pain relief. Let the tears flow and let them help to heal your heart.

The importance of structure

When I surrendered to the depression, I felt as if someone had put my life into one of those vacuum storage bags and sucked all the air out of it. I had no energy, headspace or motivation for anything else. I couldn't even focus on reading without becoming distracted. I felt like a total mess.

It's common to lack focus and to feel totally lost in the first few weeks of being single again.

Whilst it's important to surrender to the pain, it's also important to have some structure to help you keep putting one foot in front of the other. Structure helps you to continue to flow through a healing journey rather than getting stuck in a depressive rut.

So every day needs some kind of a 'plan'. As with all the steps on this journey, you need to start small. You need to decide your next steps just for today. That's it. Small, small steps such as having breakfast, planning the next meal. A daily routine helps get you through the mornings, then the afternoons, then the evenings – until you can finally get sleep, the elixir of healing.

In the darkest days of my heartbreak depression, I managed to get some structure in to create a morning routine. I often called my aunt or brother first thing. I'd cry and discuss how I was feeling. Then I'd make a pot of tea, shower, get dressed, watch a motivational video or TED Talk or listen to a podcast. That very basic structure got me through. Over the course of my years of working with those who have been floored by the pain of their heartbreak, I have come to realise how important these seemingly small steps are.

Healing from a broken heart is as much a physical process as an emotional one. Remember, it's very similar to recovering from an addiction, which is why it feels so incredibly painful. Sadly, we can't simply 'take' something or someone to make us feel better. We need to do some work to truly value ourselves and that work is facilitated by a simple structure through the darkest moments.

Without structure, depression can tip into despair and, if it all gets too much, it's common to flee to unhealthy behaviours such as bingeing (on alcohol, shopping and food) to escape the pain. Even a seemingly healthy outlet can become an obsessive way of coping if we take it to excess. Three hours a day at the gym, anyone? When many of your previous structures (within the container of the relationship with your ex) have disappeared or changed, you might feel anxious. Where is my safe place? How do I get through this? What should I do next? So, remember to start small, with a structured container of some basics of self-care.

Everyone has their own unique version of what self-care looks like. But when you're navigating the seas of feelings of depression, it's important to start with the basic 'daily resources'. These might seem obvious but I'm going to remind you about them now, as heartbreak and depression can do funny tricks to our minds and make us forget even the simplest of things.

Focusing on your daily basic resources

In the early days of grief, it's not the time for grand ambitions or for pushing yourself. Like a garden in winter, all you need to do is focus on the survival essentials. Nutrition, hydration, oxygen, exercise, sleep.

These essential resources will help you survive through the darkest moments. Start with the ones that you find easiest to do and build from there.

- **Going outside:**
Make sure you go outside at least once a day. In the depths of heartbreak, your home will feel like a personal cocoon and the temptation to stay hidden inside might be high. Going out can feel overwhelming, but this anxiety will pass with time, as you create more certainty and add variety to each day. Walking outside isn't just good for an endorphin boost, it's a great distraction from your own head and will allow you to breathe in some lovely, fresh oxygenated air.

- **Sleep:**
If you're struggling to sleep, listening to podcasts or audiobooks might help you fall asleep. Some people find that watching a late-night film or television helps to soothe them, but my recommendation is that you try to fall asleep without looking at a screen (as there is a lot of scientific data that shows how the blue light from screens can disrupt the quality of sleep). Weighted blankets can also be wonderful for reducing anxiety.

- **Exercise:**
Release those endorphins! Even if you only take a short walk every day, it will help. Put on your sunglasses, take your tissues and walk. Hide behind your sunglasses and cry to release the pain. (This is something I did daily in the early days of my heartbreak.)

- **Nutrition:**

Keeping your mind and body healthy strengthens your ability to cope. You may have completely lost your appetite, but you need to find ways to stay nourished and to stay hydrated, as these are two of the most fundamental human needs. If you've completely lost your appetite, try drinking your nutrition in smoothie or soup form.

These basic essentials will give you a healthier baseline from which you will be able to start healing. Don't underestimate the immense power of some basic self-care!

Take special care of yourself as your heart is healing. Be a good friend to yourself by putting in a bit of structure to look after yourself and try to find a little something that lifts you each day. Even if you're just going through the motions for now, that's OK. It's an important step. And you will find your sparkle again.

'The worst thing about today? I woke up.'

I once sat with a client who was in the depths of despair.
'Do you know what the worst thing about today was?' he asked.
I slowly shook my head as I invited him to tell me.
'I woke up,' he replied.

It is normal to feel like you'll never be OK again. Heartbreak can do that to you. But if you feel that you are tipping over into experiencing intense despair, complete lack of hope or even suicidal thoughts, and you feel that you have no loving friends to turn to, please seek immediate help from your doctor or from a therapist.

The world might feel like a cold and unloving place right now, but you will be amazed by how many wonderful supportive resources there are out there. Sometimes we need another human voice to help us stay strong in dark moments. My client, who had been in the clutches of despair, went on to thrive. By sharing the dark thoughts that were festering inside him and allowing me to support him through this difficult time as we worked through the pain together, he became able to reharness his resources for going from surviving to experiencing a rich and joyous life.

No matter how dark things might look, there is always light ahead. The sun will always rise. You will get through this.

Today you're going to ... prioritise your basic resources

For each of the following four statements, I'd like you to answer 'yes' or 'no':

In the last week I have ...
... been outside regularly to get some fresh air.
... got some good quality sleep.
... done some exercise.
... eaten in a way that makes me feel good.

If you said 'yes' to everything, then it's bingo – keep it up! If any of your answers were a 'no', I'd like you to write out three things that you can commit to doing over the following week, to ensure you prioritise these essential resources.

1. ....
   ....
   ....
   ....

2. ....
   ....
   ....
   ....

3. ....
   ....
   ....
   ....

6.

Starting to accept what has happened

You will find that there will be a moment when you start to find some peace around what has happened. You will 'accept' it and, from that point onwards, you will be able to move on. That might seem like a far way off right now but trust me, you will get there.

In this step, I'm going to share a very simple but important tool for overcoming a core barrier for getting to this place of acceptance. There might be a little storm of pain on the way, so bear with me on this one ...

Saying farewell to the fantasy

In the early days and weeks of heartbreak grief, it's normal to vacillate between denial and bargaining. If you've surrendered to the flow of grief and things are starting to shift, you will eventually naturally move out of this and into a place of acceptance, but sometimes there are blockages to this flow.

A common stumbling block happens when people cling to the 'fantasy' and believe that they could go back to the 'way it was'. I often have to remind clients of this and use this language—fantasy—very deliberately. It's really hard to hear, but it's really important.

Even if your ex does change - or you change - and you then get back together ... how will you rebuild the trust? It isn't impossible but it is very, very unusual for that to happen. When your heart is hurting so much, it's so hard to abandon the story.

Giving up hope and accepting what has happened is an essential step in getting unstuck. Painful, but true.

If your relationship has ended, the chances of reviving it are very low. In all my years of working with clients, it's only ever happened THREE times. Apart from those, no ex has ever come back begging for a second chance. So, unless the pair of you have explicitly discussed giving it another go, it is vital to give up this idea. If it does so happen that there is repair then, more often than not, you will find that you go back into a cycle that ends up back in another rupture.

Why you can't get closure from your ex

When people talk about recovering from heartbreak, you'll often hear the word 'closure' and this is where the stumbling block to achieving 'acceptance' comes in – from the mistaken belief that you will get closure from your ex.

Closure is the idea that we can understand the 'reasons' a relationship went wrong. After a rupture, it's something our brains are desperate to achieve. Why? Because we believe that, as a result, we will be able to accept what happened and feel a sense of resolution that will enable a fresh start.

When a relationship ends amicably, it's easier to move on and restructure your life fairly quickly. When it's an unexpected breakup, however, it can leave us in limbo and knock us so off-balance we feel we can never trust again. How could someone you thought you knew so well do this to you? Sadly, many of us land in this kind of abyss without getting closure, leaving us feeling deeply traumatised.

If this is you, you may be frantically wondering what you did wrong, constantly thinking back to when they last did or said something kind that made you feel connected to them. One client likened this process of constantly searching for answers to picking at a physical wound. (This is the bargaining stage of grief that I touched on earlier.) Here's the important thing you need to know: when a relationship ends acrimoniously, more often than not you're not going to get those answers. Whatever your ex said or did, it may never make sense.

I'm going to do a little bit of myth-busting here: the reality is that you can't get closure from your ex. The things that they say or the explanations that they give you are not going to heal you. Healing is an inside job. The work you do on *you* is going to give you the closure you so badly need. That's one of the most important things you'll get from this book. Once you have worked your way through it and done all the exercises, the door will have very firmly closed on your past. Trust me.

The ending of a relationship means the end of seeking the connection of understanding. When someone wants to end a relationship, they are not looking to get closer to you or to give you deeper insights into the inner workings of their soul.

If you are still communicating from a place of seeking connection whilst they are communicating from a place of wanting the connection to be shut down, you will not be able to meet in the middle. Your destinations and desired end points are different. You need to stop looking to 'meet in the middle' as there is no 'middle' any more.

You are both looking for different things: they are looking for reasons for you *not* to be together, whilst you are looking for connection. They have left and departed from connection. So, you will never meet in a place of understanding. By its very definition, the ending of a relationship is the end of a connection. So after a relationship is over you will not have any real access to their place of 'truth', as their future will be pointing in a different direction from yours.

You know a relationship is over when one or both of you stops being interested in evolving and in finding ways to connect, to grow together in the relationship and to learn more about how to support each other's needs and values. If someone isn't interested in growth and isn't interested in supporting you and your needs and values, then there is nothing you can do to change that. It's important to know when it's time to let go.

I once started working with a client who had been stuck in seeking closure for five years. She was still going over messages her ex had sent years before, still trying to make sense of his lies – even though he'd married someone else by then. She kept stalking him, sitting outside his house in her car, observing his life to try to make sense of her own. This was one of the most painful cases of denial I had ever witnessed. As soon as we started working together, she began to experience relief. And, as she worked her way through the steps of my structured process, she found new insights and a new understanding that led her to close the door on the past and not look back! She reached the place of acceptance ... and went on to create the most beautiful life for herself.

If your ex does not want the relationship and does not want to be with you, this is closure. You do not want to be with someone who does not value and appreciate you.

From today, close the door on the possibility that you'll be together again. You're going to stop wishing they'll contact you to say they've made a huge mistake. If you don't, you'll end up stuck.

Through the course of this book, we're going to get to the place of 'acceptance' and beyond, where you will start creating a wonderful new foundation to build on. First, let's double down on getting you out of any lingering denial or bargaining ruts, so you can create the space for the acceptance to creep in.

Today you're going to ... close the door

This exercise is to be used as an immediate response when you recognise that you have let your ex in through the door of your 'awareness' and you are back in the 'fantasy'. It's a deceptively simple exercise but is very powerful.

The exercise is this: every time your ex pops into your head and you find yourself thinking about them (whatever you are doing, whatever time of day it is), you create a mental image in your mind of a door between the two of you and then imagine yourself closing that door, so they are no longer in your mind. That's it – it's that simple.

There are different ways of doing this, depending on how you are feeling at that moment. For example, if you are feeling in a place of quiet acceptance and they pop into your head, then follow the spirit of that energy and, with dignity, mentally thank them for appearing in your mind but politely ask them to leave and gently close the mental door behind them. You may want to add a phrase that you use in your mind when you visualise closing the door behind them. Something along the lines of: 'You do not belong in my mind any more. It is time for you to go now. Goodbye.' You don't need to say this out loud (unless you really, really want to ... and are on your own, of course!)

If you are feeling angry, feel free to slam that mental door as vigorously as you need to. We're not being literal here – we are helping you set metaphorical boundaries! Again, you might want to have a phrase you use here, perhaps this time a bit firmer: 'I want to be very clear here: it is time for you to go now. Goodbye.'

The important thing in doing this exercise is making sure you honour your needs, your emotions and your headspace. You have the power. Just make sure you keep closing that door.

EVERY. SINGLE. TIME. From now onwards. Whenever you find your ex appearing in your thoughts, you need to close the door. It's really important you do this consistently. If you keep shutting the door and keep taking the steps to move on and out of the thought loops, you WILL heal.

7.

Finding meaning

You may have already started to feel a sense of relief from some of the explanations and the reassurance that, no, you are not crazy! You may have also started to feel a little more grounded as you work your way through these steps. If that's the case: excellent! Keep it up!

If that's not the case and you're still feeling completely lost and ungrounded, then that's totally normal too. In this step, we're going to give you an anchor that will give you some sense of what is to come.

Healing is not a linear process

People heal and they move through the stages of grief at different paces. There is no single calendar of healing you should expect to be following.

The most important thing is that you allow yourself to keep feeling your feelings and learn to trust the natural magic of the grieving process.

If you stay the course of this journey, and work through these 28 steps, I promise you that you will lay the foundations not just to overcome the pain but to make your life all the better for it. Seriously! By the end of this book this will all make total sense to you but, for today, I want to share something that is a fundamental part of my own core belief system.

To do that, I want to tell you a story about something that happened some 600 years ago, in ancient Japan ...

Kintsugi for the heart

In 15th-century Japan, violent military warlords had the run of the land. Legend has it that one such warlord, the tyrannical Japanese shōgun Ashikaga Yoshimasa was outraged one day to find his favourite tea bowl had been repaired with ugly metal staples. He demanded this be rectified immediately.

Using glue to bind the break wasn't an option, so his craftspeople came up with a better idea. They took the sticky sap of a local tree and lovingly followed the crooked edges with intimate precision. When they were done, they took their most precious resource, gold powder, and gently pressed it into every sticky seam.

This 'damaged' item was considered so desirable, so uniquely exquisite, the villagers started intentionally smashing their cups, their plates and their bowls – to give them an excuse to lovingly rebind their own pieces together into a 'whole' that was considered more beautiful and more precious than the unbroken original.

This new art of repair was named kintsugi, and it redefined how the world viewed imperfection. Now the unpredictable seams of the repair embodied true beauty and glorious strength, tapping into the wildly unpredictable nature and beauty of individuality.

After the desolation of the ending of my own marriage, I saw myself as a broken and irreparable shell of my former self. Yet, as I developed my structured healing system that you are working through now, the breaking open of my heart released all of the emotions, forgotten passions and hidden wants I had neglected for years, and I tapped into the 'powdered gold' that we all have banked in our soul.

It is now the seams of gold that make me, me. It is those unpredictable threads of my own path that make me infinitely strong. I've tapped into the real gold that I had within.

Your broken heart has the potential to unlock your inspired future.

I call this process kintsugi for the heart.

The courage to break from the expected

A healing journey takes great courage because it asks us to forge our own path ahead. The predictable shell of our expectations has been broken and there is no 'cookie cutter' mould to define who we are any more. We need to make decisions about how our future is going to look.

The irony is that this is the only healthy way to fully live our lives. If we sleepwalk through life without ever questioning our choices or digging deep inside to find the answers, we can only follow the pathways set by others. A fully embodied life needs us to break free from cultural shackles and the expectations of others, and to cultivate the beauty of our own inner wilderness. When our hearts break, we mend them with the gold of our true inner voice.

Gardens benefit from the winter months in a myriad of ways. The columbines, lavender and lupin seeds will only germinate in an icy snap; the alliums, crocuses and tulips need the cold to stimulate stem growth; and the Sweet Williams and Aquilegias won't flower until they have been through a cooler period. Gardens need winter to fully yield their riches and go on to thrive.

The winter fissures of your heartbreak and your journey inwards to heal will allow you to fully bloom. If you have the courage to continue to keep taking steps forward, this will be the making of you.

Today you're going to ... start to reclaim your 'you-ness'

Today, your exercise is to think of one thing you feel proud of in your heartbreak journey so far. Perhaps you kept your dignity in the midst of a difficult conversation; perhaps you stood up for yourself at an important moment; perhaps it took great courage to pick up this book or to admit your feelings to yourself ... don't discount the little things. However big or however small, write it out below.

When I was at the beginning of my heartbreak journey to healing, my proud moment was this: *I allowed myself to fully feel the pain and I surrendered to the flow of grief.*

What can you feel proud of?

. . . .
. . . .
. . . .
. . . .
. . . .
. . . .
. . . .
. . . .
. . . .
. . . .
. . . .
. . . .
. . . .
. . . .
. . . .

*Your boundaries
are your quest.*

- Rumi

Part II

TAKING ACTION:
Drawing Boundaries

In my garden in the early days of spring, before the first leafy green shoots tentatively poke their heads up out of the mucky winter soil, the clutter and debris of previous seasons needs to be cleared away. Underneath a mess of leaves that have blown in from neighbouring gardens and nearby parks, you can hardly recognise my early spring garden – it blurs in with its surroundings. Even though I know there is beauty, stirring below the surface of the soil, it feels rather unloved. Often the perimeter fence is a tiny bit damaged and the contours of the beds and paths a little fuzzy; it needs some repair.

When you are in the process of recovering from the ending of your relationship, you might still be clinging onto the past for comfort. And you might need to do some inner repair work. Change can be really hard. I understand that ... but, my lovely, it's time for us to get you properly stuck into the process of healing now. It's time to start taking some action, clearing away some of the debris of the past and reclaiming your sense of self.

Clearing out the old to make space for the new is an important step towards thriving in your consciously created world. But taking action isn't just about movement and change. It goes much deeper. It is about defining *who you are*.

I didn't know that until my heart broke.

After my first heartbreak epiphany, when I surrendered fully to the flow of grief, I immersed myself in all the feelings of denial, anger, bargaining and depression. My weary soul needed to rest and recuperate from its grief-stricken winter hibernation. Eventually, I reached the point of acceptance. Emerging from the peacefulness and feeling that I could accept the ending, I felt the first awakenings of a spring-like energy, stirring just beneath the surface. For the first time, I had the energy to take action. It was at that moment of acceptance that the next life-changing revelation flowed into my awareness – the *meaning* of all that pain crept in, all on its own. I finally started to understand *why* I had actually *needed* this rupture. When I first realised it, it was an incredible jolt to my soul.

I realised that I had lost myself.

Somehow, over the course of the years (through my childhood training, an early first marriage and then an emotional escape into a hasty second marriage), I had completely lost any sense of who I was. My true sense of self was buried under the rubble of the various roles I had been busy playing, in particular that of the 'loving wife'.

It dawned on me that the question 'who am I, without you?' was the most fundamentally important question that my soul had been begging me to answer, for years. It had been there all along, niggling in the back of mind throughout my relationships. I had batted it away over and over again. It was time for me to address it.

My entire identity had become completely enmeshed with my partner. I knew I needed to clear away the debris of the relationship and repair the perimeters of my being before I did anything else. Only then could I start to cultivate my new life and reclaim my identity.

I needed to work on my boundaries.

Let me explain ...

8.

Setting accountability boundaries

Your boundaries define who you are. They define what is yours and what is not yours.

Having good boundaries means you are taking responsibility for your own thoughts, feelings and actions. It means you are not taking responsibility for the thoughts, feelings and actions of others.

How could I have reached my forties and not known that before? And yet there I was, just starting to accept the ending of my relationship when this 'new' information hit me like a ton of bricks. It seemed like such a simple concept ... and yet my journey to get there had taken me so long.

It took the splintering of my heart into a thousand little pieces for me to realise that I was the only person in the world who could put me back together again.

In these next steps, we're going to give you the foundational tools to start to put you back together again.

The importance of accountability

My dear Aunt Vonnie (who gave me the gifts of connection, trust and safety – all things that were difficult to come by in my turbulent childhood family home), had a set of principles she lived by and instilled in me from an early age. Through these principles she taught me that *success in life is determined by how much we are able to take responsibility.* She said that it was important that we direct our energy towards the things that are in our power to change and letting go of the things that are not in our control.

I knew that.

The idea that I could no longer look to my partner to define me—that I needed to do some work on my boundaries—was palatable, and something I was excited to start learning about. It was the shadow side of that story that was the trickier part to confront: I had to acknowledge the fact that I could no longer have any influence over my ex. His choice not to be with me meant that we were, suddenly, completely separate entities. I had to stop imposing my desires onto *him.* I had to accept that I had no influence over him. Now that was a horrifically painful realisation for me.

The definition of a broken boundary is when someone imposes their own thoughts, feelings or actions on another person (whether by force, by persuasion, manipulation or coercion). Standing up for your boundaries means standing up for yourself and protecting those precious thoughts, feelings and actions: they are yours alone and nobody else has the right to claim ownership or power over them. They play a central role in defining who you are.

Anger is an important emotion as it lets you know when your boundaries are being broken. Anger is the form of energy that lets us know what is important to us and who we are. When I was in the depths of the angry stage of my grieving process, I had been so busy acknowledging my anger towards my ex that I had become a bit lost in a kind of 'victim' role. Absorbed in rageful thoughts about him and occasionally fantasising about acts of revenge meant that I was not only holding on tightly to the relationship, I was actually transgressing a boundary towards him because I had been focused on wanting *him* to change. I was putting a huge amount of emphasis and precious energy into thinking about him. It was time for me to channel my energy back into me.

That didn't mean that I didn't have the right to be angry – it simply meant that I decided to stop the habit of 'giving' all that energy away.

Putting energy into the things we can change

The foundational work of defining your boundaries is putting your energy into yourself. That means taking full responsibility for the path that lies ahead.

My many years of experience as a relationship coach have shown me that everyone heals in a different way, but I found that there is one consistent thread in everyone I have ever worked with: healing is an ACTION. It's not a philosophy.

Taking action isn't easy. Change takes a huge amount of energy. Human brains are hard-wired to seek patterns and to connect the dots on things, so we can conserve energy. That's because when patterns become habits, they take far less mental and physical energy than constantly responding to all the different things going on around us. So, one of the reasons we resist change is that change is, quite simply, exhausting.

We also resist change because, like all living beings, we are risk-averse. And change involves risk – the risk of the unknown and the risk of 'not getting it right'. The habits that have kept us 'safe' and alive until now bias us (through the inner mechanics of neural patterning in our brain) into keeping on doing those same things. Even so-called 'bad' habits are hard to change because our instincts (the habits that keep us alive) tell us to keep doing the same thing, to keep surviving.

Another big reason that change can be so painful is that we often mistake the things that we do every day with *who we are*. Our identity can be quite wrapped up in doing the things we have 'always' done or that we have, even recently, become accustomed to.

All of this makes it oh-so-hard to take even the smallest first steps towards change. I would never tell you it's easy! Right now, however, you have me alongside you, metaphorically holding your hand through it. We're going to edge forwards, together.

It's not just safe to make changes now … it's necessary.

Today you're going to ... take an active role in making changes

If you have been feeling victimised, that is totally understandable. If this is the case, I'd like to coax you into feeling motivated about taking a role of active empowerment over passive pain. You can do this!

I'd like you to think back to a time in your life when you felt powerful and like a fully embodied version of your 'best self'. Draw out a word or a symbol that represents this feeling. Even if you can only capture a fleeting sense of this feeling in your mind, that's OK. By the end of this process, you will have a strong sense of it. The important thing, for now, is to create a talisman, a kind of symbolic representation of that feeling of empowerment. When I did this exercise, I visualised an ancient oak tree, deeply rooted and profoundly grounded in the rich earth.

When you have drawn out the word or the symbol, cut out the image and put it up somewhere in your home, where you will be reminded of it. Try to take a look at it every day and remind yourself that you are not a victim – you are a powerful being, with exciting things ahead of you.

9.

Setting internal boundaries

When you are channelling your energy into your own growth, you can focus on becoming a little more discerning in the shape and tone of that energy. Are you ready to take a look at your own interior world?

Let's start that work with a 'check in'.

Checking in

How are you feeling, my lovely?

In coaching sessions, I always start by checking in. I just ask a simple question—'how are you today?'—and, in doing so, I open the space for the client to express how they are feeling.

I encourage everyone I work with to continue this habit with themselves. EVERY. SINGLE. DAY.

It's one of the most important habits you can develop in life.

A baseline of self-care

When you have clarity and have named how you are feeling, you can work out what action you need to take, in that very moment. Ask yourself 'how can I take good care of myself today?'

This practice of clarity and action will serve as a foundation for great self-care.

It is important that you prioritise taking responsibility, as well as taking care of how you feel and what you do. High standards of self-care are the starting point of boundaries.

There are some easy questions you can ask yourself to find out how good your self-care is: is the way I am treating myself how I would treat a good friend or a child I really love?; am I proud of the way I am behaving?; would I recommend this behaviour to anyone else? If the answer is 'no' to any of those questions, you might want to do a bit of work on raising your standards for yourself. Setting good internal boundaries is not always easy and there may be some barriers to overcome. (More on that, later.) But a good first step is to keep asking yourself the right questions.

A habit of journalling

Some people find that when they are in the process of recovering from heartbreak, or any form of healing journey, keeping a journal can be a helpful tool. Unlike my structured process, which is very carefully and deliberately designed to take you on a step-by-step journey, a journal gives you the possibility of a free-flowing form of expression. It can help you tune into your thoughts and feelings.

If this is something that appeals to you, I recommend you do this alongside the work you are doing in this book and that you use the journal to write out the answers to those two questions: 'How am I today?' followed by 'How can I take good care of myself today?'

Allow your pen to flow freely.

Balancing change and growth, without overwhelm

Change, growth and adaptability are the very definition of *life*. They aren't just important – they are essential elements of survival. At the same time, it's incredibly important to keep things in balance, so you don't slip into overwhelm.

'Overwhelm' means you are trying to take on too much. It's the body's mechanism for sending a message that we need to slow down. If you do find yourself feeling like it's all a bit much, then listen to that feeling. Good self-care means keeping things in balance.

Today you're going to ... stop overwhelm in its tracks

There are some lovely and simple techniques I use with my clients to help them slow down and become more embodied again, when they feel like they are slipping into overwhelm.

When it all feels too much ...

- remind yourself not to judge your feelings. You wouldn't berate yourself for feeling thirsty – you would (hopefully) instead simply allow yourself to quench the thirst by rehydrating. Any feeling of any kind should be treated in the same way. So if you feel overwhelmed, instead of passing judgement of any kind (and perhaps translating this into feeling impatient with yourself/ ashamed of your humanness/ despair that things will never get better ... and so on), take the time to explore the feeling. Ask yourself the question we covered earlier: 'How can I take good care of myself today?'

- write out a list of everything that you are feeling afraid of, stressed or anxious about; anything you don't have enough time for. Sometimes the act of just putting it down onto paper can really help.

- allow yourself some time to zone out. Do whatever feels relaxing to you and whatever enables you to switch off that whirring mind of yours. Relaxation is not a waste of time – it is a very important part of self-care. Remember to be kind to yourself. You are on an important journey. Sometimes journeys take time.

10.

Setting physical boundaries

This next step is a really practical one, with some important emotional implications. We're going to shake up the rooms in which you live, and breathe fresh life back into them. We're going to do a declutter. As with all the steps, it's important you complete this one.

Why we're clearing

Creating internal change takes time, repetition, great guidance, clarity and vision. When you create the right environment for change, you teach your brain that it's not only 'safe' to change, it can also build energising momentum.

Reclaiming your home space after a breakup isn't a wishy-washy meaningless self-help tool, it is a means of resetting your physical (environmental) boundaries. This declutter will allow you to …

- **Remove any 'triggers'**
Having constant reminders of your ex in your home environment will keep pulling you back mentally to thinking about them.

- **Get any lingering 'reasons to contact your ex' out of the way**
It's important to get rid of anything that might tempt you to stay a little bit stuck in any fantasies of rekindling the relationship.

- **Lay the foundations for your new life**

As you start to gently make space for your new life, you are laying the foundations for some of the next waves of work. (Remember that changes are made through repetition and gradually building ... more of that to come, soon!)

Today you're going to ... declutter your living space

For this exercise you are going to need three boxes. (If you don't have those to hand, don't delay doing the exercise – you can create three piles instead until you have had a moment to source the boxes. Just make sure you don't delay too long, as this step is an important part of your healing journey.) You are going to go room to room in your house and sort into these three boxes anything that is in any way related to your ex. You are going to need to make choices about which of the three boxes these things will go into ...

1. The 'GIVE BACK' box

This is going to be the easiest box to fill. It is for anything that belongs to them that you want to give back. Once you've packed up their things, you'd ideally get them out of your home as soon as possible. You might prefer to meet them in person or it may be easier to post the things back to them. (My recommendation is never to pull in a friend or family member to do this – it may seem tempting to get the extra support, but this kind of 'triangulation' is often counterproductive and adds an unnecessary layer of complication.)

2. The 'LET GO' box

This box is for all reminders of your ex. Add anything that reminds you of your ex in any way. The photographs, the gifts your ex gave you or the things you bought together … it's a good idea to remove anything that makes you feel as if your heart is being ripped out when you look at it. Take this 'LET GO' box to a local charity shop if you can. You may, like me, get a lovely sense of satisfaction knowing that someone else is going to get great use out of the things that no longer serve you – sending out a nice little bit of love into the world! If you don't have a local charity shop, then put it in the garbage. The important thing is that it is out of your home. You need to clear space for your new life.

3.   The 'TREASURE?' box

This box is for anything you consider valuable (either in terms of their monetary value or in terms of emotional value), that you aren't yet ready to get rid of. We're adding a '?' to the name of this box, as you might not be in the best place to make decisions about it, right now. This will be a box that you store in a safe space or ask a trusted friend or family member to keep for you, until you are able to decide what to do with the items. Write a note in your diary a year from now, to remind you to take a look at the 'TREASURE?' When you do eventually examine the contents again, with the perspective of a clearer head, you'll be able to make an easier judgement about what to do with it. You may find at this stage you have a level of indifference and that this will no longer be a painful thing to address. In the early days of an ending, emotional turmoil can often hinder our perspective, leaving us less equipped to be able to make these decisions.

How to work out what goes where

I remember a time after my divorce when a close girlfriend of mine told me I should get rid of all the jewellery an ex had given me because it had 'bad energy'. Well, I don't agree with this –

71

it's how you feel about things and the meaning you give them that counts. If you feel strongly about no longer keeping these items, then you can decide what will be best to do with them (sell them, gift them, donate them ... whatever works for you) but if you want to hold onto them there's nothing wrong with that.

I wasn't able to wear the jewellery from my ex for many years after the ending of our relationship. But when the memories transformed and I found myself feeling grateful for what I had learnt from our time together, I found I was able to wear this jewellery fondly. My wedding ring was another story altogether. As much as I loved the design and treasured the ring, I could no longer wear it because it symbolised something sacred that had ended. I changed the design and created a new ring that I gifted to my daughter for her birthday.

It's a personal decision you need to make. It is all about what it 'means', to *you*.

An extended declutter

When I've worked through this exercise with clients, I've often found that they are inspired to do a deeper, more prolonged declutter of their home.

If you were with your ex for a long time, your lives may have been physically intertwined. You may have shared a home together but, even if you weren't at that stage yet or don't have any physical reminders of them in your home, the space represented the version of you that you were *then*. We're now creating the backdrop for your fresh start.

A breakup is the perfect time to get rid of anything that doesn't feel either BEAUTIFUL or USEFUL in your life. If it has no meaning and no value to you, there's no point in holding onto it. (If you'd like a detailed and structured process, you might find the work of Marie Kondo really helpful here. I have also found Helen Sanderson's *Home Declutter Kit* very useful.)

Rearranging the furniture, so that the rooms feel different and organised the way you like them, can be a great way of bringing in a wave of new energy. (If you don't have space to move furniture around, you can put some different pictures on the wall instead.) As you're doing this, see if you can let yourself start to think about what you'd love to bring more of into your home and start to envision your new life ahead.

Be prepared that this physical clearing work might stir up some emotional turbulence. That's expected and OK. It's all part of the process. Notice your feelings and take positive action to support yourself as you are doing this.

11.

Setting mental boundaries

Once you have decluttered your living space from traces of your ex and have given them back anything that belonged to them, you are in a place to set mental boundaries.

Going no contact

When you leave a relationship, you may find yourself struggling with fully separating and differentiating your thoughts (from the place of 'we' to 'I') and reclaiming your boundaries. This is particularly hard for those who are emerging from codependent or enmeshed relationships, but it applies to everyone.

Remember, in Step 6, when we talked about 'closure'? Closure comes from within and cutting contact gives you the space to withdraw from the chemical attachment your brain is craving.

If you don't share children or a business, I recommend that you set the intention to make no contact for at least three months. After that, if you still crave connection, you might want to make this last a little longer. The idea is that you set a boundary for yourself to ensure that you will not be in contact with them until you no longer wish to be in a partnership with them (and are in a place of wanting a genuine friendship, without any lingering feelings of physical attraction). In some cases, it's eventually possible to be friends with your ex but ONLY if you feel uninterested in them (once the oxytocin connection goes). And, to break this bond, you need to cut contact.

Best-case scenario? You both decide to disconnect from each other.

Cutting contact will speed up the healing process.

Delete and block

It sounds radical but it really helps.

Once you delete their number, you can't keep checking when they last WhatsApped.

When you delete the old messages, you can eliminate 'coping fatigue', where you're constantly picking at that wound. Messages, photos, texts, voice notes, letters from your ex … all these things that live inside your virtual 'home' territories (on your phone, computer, email or social media accounts) can also be triggers.

The one thing my clients always say they feel when they finally block and delete is RELIEF. You can breathe deeper. The compulsion stops and healing begins.

After a breakup, it's so easy to mine social media for endless details about what your ex is doing now. The brain goes into overdrive seeking what it's lost, and this can spill into cyber-stalking. Dwelling on their 'happy new life without you' can make you feel like your heart's being ripped out. If you happen to see them with their new partner in person, it's a billion times worse! Brooding about all the things you did together—which they now do together—can drag your self-worth down to a very dark place.

In some ways, being dumped by my second husband felt worse than dealing with my first husband's death. When someone dies, there's no more bargaining you can do. It's over. But it was painful seeing my ex move on as I struggled with heartache. And it's because I felt stuck that I understand how to stop you getting stuck.

So block social contact, delete the possibilities of staying connected to them.

If they really need to reach you, there's always a way.

Firm boundaries when contact is complicated

This is a tough one. In an ideal world, when a relationship is over, you or they can move out and start to move on. But, in reality, that's not always an immediate practical possibility for some. So you are going to need to pay a lot of attention to maintaining healthy boundaries. If you have no choice but to live in the same home, set up your own sleeping and even living area. If that's not possible, then ensure that you are spending time outside the home as well—it isn't helpful to continue on 'as normal' as though nothing has changed—it can slow down your healing.

Keep things respectful but ideally keep a detached distance – don't get tempted to seek connection or closeness in these early stages of nursing your heartbreak. Think of them as a kind of 'housemate/ work colleague' and try to use this frame to avoid the temptation towards intimacy of any kind.

Sometimes you don't have the luxury of deleting and blocking your ex because ties connect you, such as children or a business. Transitioning from a couple to co-parents or colleagues can be more complex than you expect. You need to sort out custody logistics, financial arrangements and, above all, protect the hearts of your children.

This is when boundaries matter, so be honest about your own and respect your ex's. There's no place for emotion in these negotiations.

Now's not the time to talk over the past, try to get answers or check how they're spending their free evenings.

Whilst it may be complicated to maintain privacy, whilst you heal, there are certain things you can do to support yourself.

Remember: boundaries are about what *you* do and how *you* behave. Whilst you can assert your preferences and request certain standards be met, you can only enforce this by the actions that you take, as anything else would (by very definition) be boundary-breaking for the other people involved.

Today you're going to ... delete and block

OK. Deep breath in and deep breath out. Today you are going to delete their number, block social media contact and then get rid of those digital reminders (messages, photos, texts, voice notes etc.). If you're really struggling to get rid of these in one go, get a memory stick and download them all for you to consider getting rid of at a later date. Label the memory stick and put it away, in storage, inside your box marked 'TREASURE?'

12.

Setting boundaries with the wider world

If you have been with your ex for some time or if you work together, it's helpful to have some strategies mapped out for yourself and to keep things crystal clear in your own mind, to avoid being drawn into any emotional situations. In this step we're going to review some of the things you can do to ensure you maintain healthy wider boundaries.

It's complicated

Where others are involved, there are some specific things you can bear in mind for different scenarios ...

- **At work: Keep it strictly business**
What if you and your ex have a clear no-contact rule, but work for the same company? Agreeing exactly how you're going to coexist within the workplace can be really helpful for your happiness and peace of mind. More importantly (and in cases where you can't talk to your ex), you need to set those standards yourself.

- **With your ex's friends & family: Avoid too much information**
You may be close to members of their family or wider circle. While it's possible to maintain this kind of connection, you need to make it clear to them that you don't want your chats to stray into discussing how your ex is doing.

- **With friends: Limit gossip**

Well-meaning pals may want to share information about your ex's new life. Even if you're dying to hear the gritty details ... please don't get drawn in. It's like being dragged underwater when you want to breathe freely. Rather, tell friends how hard you're working to move on and ask them to skip the subject so you can heal. Bad-mouthing or manipulating a situation to show your ex up as Voldemort isn't an option either. If you need to explain, the ideal one-liner is: *We had different values.* Because this IS generally the reason for an ending. One person wants commitment and something to change, the other doesn't. One values something or someone else more than the other. Whatever the reason was, that one-liner lets you offer the perfect explanation without going into detail.

At some point in the future ...

As you settle into new lives, perhaps with new partners, things will change. Boundaries can be renegotiated. What matters is that they are clear and defined. Over time, it might be possible to build a kind, respectful and long-lasting new friendship with your ex.

I know that sometimes this is not what happens. Sometimes an ex is hell-bent on vengeance. A friend of mine endured a costly and emotionally draining legal process when her ex was determined to prove her an unfit mother, though the judge disallowed his claim. Another client fought through multiple issues, from custody battles for his kids to property sale disputes, on and on and on. But each was resolved and the relief was WONDERFUL.

If you need to be in contact with your ex but they are behaving badly, hang in there. You can't change their approach. All you can do is respond neutrally, consider putting all communication in writing and stick to the facts. Make sure you have support. If friends and family are not enough, seeing a therapist weekly can really help you navigate the storm.

And know this ... you can't change them, but you CAN change the way you interact with them. You don't need to get sucked in. With practice, your boundaries can get stronger and stronger, as you find your sense of self again.

Today you're going to ... anticipate any pitfalls ahead

When we take things out into the sunlight, from the dark recesses of the shadows, they lose some of their mysterious powers. Our imaginations are calmed when we are faced with the pragmatics of realities. So giving shape to the things that are worrying us and defining them by capturing and naming the loose threads of thoughts that whirr around them, takes away the possibility of them running amok in our minds.

What boundary pitfalls are you concerned about? How can you take measures to prevent any of these pitfalls from happening? Write out everything you are worried about, as you start to do your work of putting good boundaries in place, and everything you can do to support yourself with them.

. . . .

. . . .

. . . .

. . . .

. . . .

. . . .

. . . .

. . . .

. . . .

. . . .

. . . .

. . . .

. . . .

13.

Clarifying boundaries from the inside out

When life has shaken you to your very core and you have felt fragmented and broken (whether through a gradual wearing down over time or through a life-shattering sudden rupture), it's easy to lose sight of who you really are, at your core. Things can feel very out of alignment. As though the broken pieces of you are sitting in a muddled pile – unrecognisable as a whole. Part of putting your life back in order is getting these pieces back in their rightful place. As you start to get clearer about defining and taking responsibility for the garden of your own inner world, you start to reclaim your full sense of self.

In this step, we're going to take a look at your core 'values' – the standards that articulate what is important to you.

Values strengthen boundaries and define needs

Every individual on the planet has a unique hierarchy of things that are important to them. Even if you don't know it, these 'core values' are part of the very fabric of your being and have a strong guiding influence on the trajectory of your life. When you take actions in alignment with your values, life flows freely. Decisions are clearer because your guiding principles are at the forefront.

Getting really clear about your values is a fundamentally important thing that helps in all aspects of day-to-day life. Your values will be signposts showing the direction of knowing what makes you happy and what you need. When you know your own values, decisions about life become easier because you are less at risk of being manipulated or prioritising the needs of others over your own. In that way, clarity on your values helps you to define and maintain boundaries between yourself and others.

Getting clarity on your values

In my work as a relationship coach, I often find that my clients don't really know what their values are. We all take for granted that we have values ... but often don't necessarily really know exactly what our core values are. Clients might think they have a rough idea or they might be able to throw out some words when asked the question ... but when we go into any exercises on getting full clarity, they are often surprised by the results.

So what, exactly, are values?

Our personal values are the things that we hold most dear in our lives. They are the standards or founding principles on what means the most to us. Even when we are not conscious about exactly what our values are, they are the foundations that define how we interact with the world. In some ways you could say that core values are our most important 'needs' that we would always prioritise above anything else – the consistent needs that form a defining part of our lives, regardless of our mood or the external circumstances.

Values are defined by where you choose to put your energy, time, focus and the needs underlying that. So, one of the best ways to understand what you really value is to take a look at what you are doing, day to day, and reverse engineer an understanding of what your values are from that.

Weeding out misalignments

If you imagine your values as a code for the set of principles that define how you make judgements about what has a rightful place in the garden of your soul and what is not welcome, you can keep an eye out for the pesky weeds that will need to be eviscerated! Some of those weeds are easy to identify whilst others might have deep roots that have been embedded from your childhood days or hangovers left behind from your ex. Don't let those weeds live rent-free in your space. Identify them and uproot them.

There's often a difference between values we believe we should have – and values we actually do have. That disconnection, where we are in denial about a part of ourselves and instead put on a 'false identity', is a form of dissociation that stops us from feeling really good about who we are and having the confidence to express who we are to others.

Be mindful of the disconnect between aspirations and actions. Is there anything that you spend a lot of time thinking about or talking about but don't spend any time doing or prioritising? If you find that you spend a lot of time thinking about something but that you don't spend a lot of time actually investing in it (whether that's an investment of time or money), it may be an indicator that you are living out of alignment with your values. For example, you might find that you spend a lot of time thinking about health and about ways to improve your health but that in practice you take very little exercise. If that's the case, it's worth having a think about whether you are not being true to yourself by committing to your health. In some cases, a disconnect relates to an externally imposed value (coming from your culture or the people around you) of a false identity. As always, clarity on what's coming from you and what isn't, is incredibly helpful.

Whenever you look at your values, have a think about what the underlying motivators might be. That will help you with your weeding. I recently did the values exercise with a client who found that most of what he thought were his values actually were masks for *deeper* needs. He thought that *leadership* and *success* were his highest values. When we dug deeper, he started to connect the dots with his past and to understand how, when he was a young boy, he had never felt fully seen, heard or acknowledged. He realised that it was actually all about *connection*. He wanted to be a leader because it allowed him to connect with people and he wanted success because the admiration that it brought made him feel connected with those admiring him.

These days, I live in total alignment with my values. My family and home life, my career, my friendships and all the other areas in which I invest my energy are all based on these core values. I am unshakeable in my resolve to protect and maintain them and they drive all of my decisions. With some careful weeding out of false identities and disconnects, I have come to know that my personal core values (in priority order) are: *connection; growth/ personal development; making a difference; health and stability (financial and emotional).*

Are you ready to get some sharp clarity on the values that define who you are?

Today you are going to ... get crystal clear on your values

I'm going to take you through an exercise that is going to help you get a fresh perspective on your values. This exercise, which I have adapted and shortened from *The Heart of Love* by Dr John Demartini, was introduced to me by my very first coach Sue Lindsay who was a Demartini facilitator. The exercise is divided into two parts.

Part 1: Where are you focusing your energy?

Write out the answers to the questions below. For each of these questions, try to be as honest as possible. This isn't for anyone other than you. The real value will come if you unearth the things that have the most energetic charge for you.

1. **What do you spend a lot of time thinking about?** (What are your fears and concerns? What dreams, plans and longings occupy your mind?)

   . . . .

   . . . .

2. **What do you talk about with others?** (What are the main themes of your conversations?)

   . . . .

   . . . .

3. **How do you spend your time and energy?** (How much time do you allocate to your work, hobbies, family or exercise?)

   . . . .

   . . . .

4. **How do you spend your money?** (Look at your monthly expenses and purchases and analyse where you spend your money.)

   . . . .

   . . . .

5. **Where in life are you most disciplined and organised?** (What are your priorities and what is most important to you?)

   . . . .

   . . . .

6. **Look around your living space – what have you filled your space with?** (This question is best answered after you have done a full declutter of your home. What is important to you in your home?)

. . . .

. . . .

Part 2: Identify the main themes

On the basis of your answers to the questions, circle all of the words in the list that you think might embody some of your values – the words that represent the essential qualities that are most important to you in your life.

You will find that there are some words that come up consistently and clearly – there is no debating their importance to you and you know that if these things didn't exist in your life you would not be living a very happy life. Of these consistent and clear front-runners, write out your top five. The things that, through the years and through your life, have always been important to you – the words that give you a little frisson of 'feeling right' and that make you feel happy to think about. These are your 'core values'. They are the essential elements of who you are. We're going to be using them in some of the next steps, to create the foundations of your vision for your future.

Reminder: in this book we've occasionally touched on how difficult it can be to lean in to the question 'who am I, without you?' When you're assessing your core values, this can be one of those moments. Sometimes the greatest rewards come out of the greatest challenges – this may well be one of those moments for you.

☐ Abundance	☐ Curiosity	☐ Learning
☐ Acceptance	☐ Decisiveness	☐ Love
☐ Accomplishment	☐ Desire	☐ Making a difference
☐ Achievement	☐ Eagerness	☐ Optimism
☐ Adaptability	☐ Enthusiasm	☐ Order
☐ Adventure	☐ Excitement	☐ Participation
☐ Affection	☐ Faithfulness	☐ Passion
☐ Balance	☐ Focus	☐ Peace
☐ Beauty	☐ Freedom	☐ Positivity
☐ Admiration	☐ Friendliness	☐ Power
☐ Being valued	☐ Friendship	☐ Purpose
☐ Belonging	☐ Fun	☐ Respect
☐ Collaboration	☐ Generosity	☐ Romance
☐ Comfort	☐ Growth	☐ Security
☐ Commitment	☐ Happiness	☐ Self-expression
☐ Communication	☐ Health	☐ Self-fulfilment
☐ Community	☐ Honesty	☐ Sensitivity
☐ Compassion	☐ Humour	☐ Sensuality
☐ Competence	☐ Independence	☐ Sincerity
☐ Competition	☐ Influence	☐ Significance
☐ Comradeship	☐ Integrity	☐ Spirituality
☐ Confidence	☐ Intelligence	☐ Stability
☐ Connection	☐ Intimacy	☐ Success
☐ Contribution	☐ Kindness	☐ Support
☐ Courage	☐ Knowledge	☐ Tranquillity
☐ Creativity	☐ Leadership	☐ Warmth

14.

Using boundaries and values to set standards

We're going to close off our work on boundaries by tapping into your values, to define the 'standards' you set for yourself in your life. From honing in on these value foundations, we'll then be able to shift gear into the beautifully enriching work that will start to unleash your fiery potential.

Calling on your 'Front Row Friends'

When you are in the process of grieving and resetting, in weeks and months ahead, you need to surround yourself with care by connecting to people you trust and who make you feel safe. I call those friends my 'Front Row Friends'. Most of us have one or more of those trusted people, the loyal pals who've got our back, never judge, and inspire us when we can't see the wood for the trees.

When my marriage broke down, my friend Lynda came to stay because I just wasn't coping with the empty space. Lynda added the sparkle and grounding I so badly needed. We'd walk the dog, morning and afternoon, and I'd say the same things, over and over. And ... she listened. She was right there, going through everything with me, a wonderful soulmate.

I found bank holidays a really difficult time to be on my own, so I invited friends, family and even their dogs over for those long weekends.

Though I didn't have much energy, I felt safe spending time with them. Real friends will love you through your grief.

If, however, you are feeling alone and isolated and there is absolutely nobody you want to spend time with, don't despair. When you are feeling low you won't have the energy for negative influences around you. That form of sensitivity can be a powerful way of getting clarity about who is a healthy person for you to have in your life and who isn't. This discernment will be another foundational skill for the next phase of your life, when you will have the tools to cultivate great connections with the kind of people who are deserving of your fabulous presence. In the meantime, I am here with you, and I will get you to that place.

We're going to harness this sensitivity to do some standard setting.

Now is the time to set a high bar

When it comes to friends, now more than ever, make sure you apply the healthy principle of KEEPING A HIGH BAR. What I mean by that is: seek the ones who encourage you and leave you feeling better after you see them. If someone is making you feel uncomfortable about your grief, you may want to give them a wide berth. In fact, if someone is making you feel uncomfortable about anything, it is a good moment to take a look at whether or not you share the same values.

If values are at the core of who you are, you do not want to be around anyone who creates a fundamental value-conflict for you. This is where the nuance of boundaries, values and standards comes into play: the most important part of setting standards for who you have around you in your life is that the people who you hold dear don't ask you to be anything other than true to your own values.

As I worked through my own heartbreak grief and did some deep inner work, using my values to review the standards I had been living by, I realised that I had been in the habit of sacrificing my values for the sake of holding onto people. There were a few people around me who were not just uncomfortable with my grief, they didn't seem to want me to evolve and deepen my own growth journey. My focus on personal development made them uneasy and they didn't like the fact that I was changing.

It became increasingly clear to me that I wanted to connect with people who were connected to their own inner worlds and who were interested in looking within to create growth and personal development. When I became clear about my own inner standards, I naturally drifted away from those people.

Now you are clear on your own core values, you can use that clarity to make sure that you are living a life in alignment with those values by setting out your own standards.

Today you're going to … translate your values into standards

Your standards are commitments you make to yourself about who you choose to keep in your life or invite into your life, in alignment with your values.

I'd like you to take the core values you defined for yourself in the previous exercise and turn these into a clear set of 'standards' you are committing to when it comes to other people. For each of the core values you are going to write out the sentence:

In order to honour my value of <write out the value>, I am committing to <doing this>.

Here are the standards I set out for myself:

* *In order to honour my value of connection, I am committing to* surrounding myself with people I feel close and connected to.

* *In order to honour my value of growth/personal development, I am committing to* spending my time with people who care about growth and personal development, who have an open and curious nature.

* *In order to honour my value of making a difference, I am committing to* seeking out people who inspire me to live in alignment with my purpose.

* *In order to honour my value of health, I am committing to* avoiding anyone who compromises my health in any way (whether mentally or physically).

What are your standards going to be for your new life?

....
....
....
....
....
....
....
....
....
....
....
....
....
....
....
....
....
....
....
....
....
....
....
....
....
....
....
....
....

*To plant a garden is to
believe in tomorrow.*

- Audrey Hepburn

Part III

FINDING SUNSHINE:
Enjoying Life Again

When I was in the process of healing from my heartbreak, there were four clear turning points for me. I've shared two of them with you already – the first was the moment I allowed myself to surrender to the power of the grieving process and the second was when I understood the concept of boundaries and used clarity, insight and knowledge of my values to stop the damaging winds of the influence of my ex and the outside world from disrupting my sense of self.

Those two big junctures had brought in an easy sense of tranquillity. A soothing balm for my soul. I had found a kind of peacefulness that was unfamiliar to me.

Whilst that peacefulness was a comfortable place to be in, as it brought me a sense of relief, I also knew that something big was missing.

It was back in my garden that I had the third major turning point.

The poor rose that I'd chopped into bits in my early days of grief hadn't been the only casualty of my heartbreak. I had done a very over-thorough 'declutter'. As spring was edging into summer, I was standing in front of a kind of blank canvas. The garden was in a state of raw readiness. The soil was open and nourished, the weeds were out, but there was very little growing. I needed to start again and to replant. I should have felt a sense of joy at the prospect but instead I felt anxious. The emptiness felt eerie. Oppressive.

That was when another of those delicious moments of enlightenment dawned on me, like the parting of clouds to reveal a pure ray of sunshine: it was the first moment in my life when I was in the position of creating, just to please *myself*. In the course of my life, I had gone straight from my childhood home into my first marriage and then hastily into my second, without ever really creating a world for myself. Everything had always been designed around the needs of everyone around me. My parents, my husband, my children ... I had, in my previously unboundaried manner, always tried to create a beautiful canvas of a setting for their life. I had always harnessed the fire of their dreams and desires to drive my creativity.

It was now time for me to look within and to act as the life-giving force for my own life. I didn't need to look outside to find the sunshine in my world – I needed to look to the light that came from within.

My own light had been dimmed so overpoweringly in my childhood that it was often no more than a barely perceptible flicker. For a long time, I didn't even know I had that fire inside me. I thought my job was to be the moon and that I existed to reflect back the glory of all the suns around, which I orbited (who cast their long shadows over me).

My 'caregivers' had carried such bruised hearts that they barely had the inner resources to keep themselves afloat, let alone enough to overflow out to support the little presence they had brought into the world. These hungry spirits, frozen in the tracks of their own childhood traumas, needed me to be their parent. So, like so many children of trauma, I parented my parents and unwittingly gave myself over to their requirements. I forgot that there was a fire in me that needed to be tended.

I needed to reignite the fire in my own world.

My lovely, it's now time for you too to mine some of those gold sunshiny threads that will bind everything together and get you ready for your phoenix-like regeneration.

Strengthened by the restorative power of grief and with increasing clarity around the perimeter boundaries of the garden of your own identity (having weeded out the presence of your ex), it is time to allow in some warmth. As you start to strengthen your foundations, you will find that the warmth will start to grow, day by day. There will be a moment when, like me, you will realise that you have a vibrant forcefield inside you. The kintsugi gold is the light that comes from you.

We're going to start sowing the seeds of your enchanted life ahead—the life that is your birthright to claim—the life in which you are not just surviving but thriving.

There will be some more deep work ahead and the time will come for deeper digging. Right now, though, it is time for some creativity, some adventure and some play.

You are ready for this.

15.

The heat of curiosity

We're now going to reignite your inner core of fire, starting slowly: with a little spark.

Follow the 'heat'

Where grief is a powerful river that sweeps you into its current and carries you and holds you through the journey towards healing, curiosity is the paddle on a canoe – it's an active and charged energy that drives you forwards and strengthens the fiery core of who you are.

Curiosity is anything but passive – when you feel a sense of curiosity you know that the energy inside you is bubbling up again and breathing new fire into your being.

Anything that piques your curiosity is precious and worthy of exploration. It is a guiding force, telling you where to focus your resources. Listen carefully to that energy.

Coaches and therapists often talk about 'hot' topics. What they mean by that is where there is an energetic focus. Your emotions are generally the best guiding force to bring awareness to what is important to you, so tune into your feelings and what they are telling you about where the energetic trail of breadcrumbs might take you. Allow your curiosity to focus on the things you feel strongly about.

Curiosity builds connection

In my work as a relationship coach for couples, I always use curiosity as a tool for reinstilling connection. By encouraging each half of the couple to get curious about what is going on for the other, they can become fully 'present' with each other - rather than just running through engrained programmes of assumptions and projections. And the exact same principles apply to really getting to know your own *self*. There are many things that you might just 'take for granted' about yourself ... but what happens if you take a look with fresh eyes? What happens if you look inwards with curiosity? You'll find that a life fully lived is one that makes space for open-hearted exploration.

Are you ready to ignite some energy? Join me in this exercise ...

Today you're going to ... ignite a spark

Close your eyes for a moment and take yourself into the hidden recesses of your mind. Is there anything, lurking there in the dark corners of your mind, that you have always longed to explore? Is there anything that you have never dared put energy or time into because it just felt too outlandish/ too unrealistic/ too far outside the realms of your experience? Holding that thought in your mind, I'd like you to write down the answers to the following questions ...

• Why do you think you long for this? What does it represent for you?

. . . .

. . . .

. . . .

. . . .

. . . .

. . . .

. . . .

. . . .

. . . .

. . . .

. . . .

. . . .

. . . .

. . . .

- How do you think doing this or experiencing this would make you feel?

....
....
....
....
....
....
....
....

- Why are those feelings important?

....
....
....
....
....
....
....
....

- What is holding you back from exploring this now?

....
....
....
....
....
....
....
....

- Could you consider giving yourself permission to continue to explore this further? Why/ why not?

. . . .

. . . .

. . . .

. . . .

. . . .

. . . .

. . . .

. . . .

There are no right or wrong answers here. And no heavy commitments or work to do: we're just acknowledging and bringing out into the daylight some of your hidden curiosities and, buried within them, your hidden dreams.

When I first did this exercise two things popped up. One was salsa dancing and the other was writing a book – yes, the very one you are either listening to or holding in your hand right now! If you enjoyed the exercise you might want to repeat it from time to time, to see what you unearth.

16.

Creating a vision for your radiant life ahead

Building on the clarity you will now have about your core values and the early flickers of the fire of curiosity you might be feeling in your soul, we are going to start to take a look at your vision for your new life ahead.

Widening your vision for your life ahead

In the early stages of heartbreak, your tunnel vision will have kept your field of focus and your sense of possibility so small that you might not have been able to visualise a happy future for yourself. Your vision of your future may also have been entirely wrapped up in your relationship with your ex, leaving behind a big, gaping void. Now the relationship is over, so too is the old vision we had with this person, and our dreams with them in our future.

If you've managed to do all the exercises in the book so far, you will already have started to feel a sense of energy stirring. You will also start to have a sense of possibility about what lies ahead, rather than continuing to go round in circles only able to look at the past. (Although that's not to say that you shouldn't be looking back at all – remember that's all part of the grieving process and you should be gentle in allowing grief to take its natural course.)

When you are processing an experience that is in any way painful, it's normal for all of your energy to get sucked in. Up until now your heart might only have been able to focus on the ending of your relationship, and the lack of this significant other in your life – the emptiness of the 'relationship' area of your life. We want to get you focused on exploring all the areas of life, from a new perspective. A perspective that is based on your values and your own vision for yourself.

It's time for you to spread your wings a little.

A vision will fan the flames

Creating a vision of the future isn't a whimsical and pointless exercise. Nor is it a way of 'teasing' the mind about what it doesn't (yet) have: it is an important step towards actively creating a life you want to have. The job it does is to give you a bit of clarity around your heart's true, unfettered desires – what you really want from life. If we can't even imagine something, it will feel completely 'off limits' to our brain.

If you actively create a vision of what you want from life, you are far more likely for that vision to come to fruition, with your focused attention pointing in that direction, looking for possibilities to make that vision happen. It's not 'magical thinking' (as it is a proven psychological phenomenon) even though the results can feel wondrously magical when your dreams do start taking flight!

In the same way that I stood in front of my spring garden, ready to sow the seeds of my future life, your vision sets the blueprint for your life ahead.

Your 'seven pairs of wings'

There are many areas of life where we express ourselves and where we have the possibility to be ourselves, to explore, to learn and to live in alignment with our values. In my work, I hone in on seven of these areas, which I call your 'seven pairs of wings'.

Romantic relationships are a subsection of just one of these seven areas. A romantic relationship is important but it's time for us to put some visionary focus into the other areas too.

Your 'seven pairs of wings' are:

1. Connection (Relationships/ Family/ Friends)
2. Health
3. Emotion
4. Spirituality
5. Personal Development
6. Career
7. Finances

With these seven areas in mind, I'd like you to come with me on a thought experiment for a moment – a soaring flight of the imagination.

Today you're going to ... ask yourself the 'miracle question'

When you think about the seven areas of your life, what is your soul longing for? What would you love to have in your life ahead? How can you bring your core values to life in these areas? In this exercise we're going to do some visioning to help you to create a mental image of how you would love your life to look.

I'd like you to imagine that tonight, as you are sleeping, a huge miracle occurs and you wake up tomorrow, and everything in your life is exactly the way you would like it to be. How would you know that a miracle had taken place?

There are many ways you can do this exercise. I suggest that you do it with words, writing out a description of your miracle life. You can also create a 'vision collage' by cutting out pictures, photos and headlines, and putting them all together as a visual embodiment of your heart's desires.

Whichever way you do it, include something from each of the seven areas of life, so you are focusing on all life areas. Be as expansive and as wild as you can with your desires—this is an exercise in stretching your imagination, not an exercise in practical and pragmatic planning—as your vision will evolve over time.

As you write out and create a collage of this miracle life, ask yourself ...

- What would you see, feel and hear that would let you know you have woken up to your miracle life?

. . . .
. . . .
. . . .
. . . .

- Where are you?

. . . .
. . . .
. . . .
. . . .

- Who is with you? How do you feel when you're with them?

. . . .
. . . .
. . . .
. . . .

- What are you planning to do today?

. . . .
. . . .
. . . .
. . . .

- What have you always wanted to be, do or have, that you have in your miracle life?

. . . .
. . . .
. . . .
. . . .

- What do you now have more time for in this life?

....
....
....
....

- What do you love?

....
....
....
....

- What makes your life enjoyable?

....
....
....
....

- What are you truly passionate about?

....
....
....
....

- What message of love would you like to leave the world?

....
....
....
....

- What creates true joy for you?

....
....
....
....

- What makes you proud?

....
....
....
....

- What makes you laugh?

....
....
....
....

- What are you truly thankful for?

....
....
....
....

- What are the beautiful, positive emotions you are experiencing?

....
....
....

17.

Resetting the stage

Now you have imagined a beautiful 'miracle' life, you are going to start to set the stage for beginning that new life.

By setting the stage for the things in life that you want, the energy of your world will be pointing towards the things you want in the future, rather than carrying the stagnant traces of the past.

Adding (metaphorical) warmth and colour to your home

Back in Step 10, you cleared the remnants of your ex out of your home. You may also have done a deeper declutter. As you start to move on and to shape the direction your life is now heading in, it's a good moment to start to think about how you want your home setting to look and to feel.

You may not be in the mood or financial space to spend a lot of money on redecorating, but giving your home space a bit of a spruce-up is an excellent thing to do after a breakup. Little details can make a big difference in moving on. New plants bring in a fresh kind of energy and life. New pictures on the wall can help take your imagination to new places.

If you have the financial means, it is worth considering getting yourself a set of new sheets. Even if your ex has never shared your bed, it's the place where you do your dreaming and a lot of your rest and recovery … so it's lovely to turn this into a beautiful oasis for yourself.

What else can you do to your home, to shape it into the setting for your new life? In your 'miracle question' visioning, perhaps you envisaged a life ahead where you looked after yourself better and your home was a kind of sanctuary, protecting you from the world. Perhaps you imagined yourself with a new partner, enjoying quiet moments together sitting in front of a fire.

When I created my own vision for my life ahead, I had this very clear image of a beautiful pergola in my garden, covered with flowers and a beautifully set table with candles, amazing food and a group of close friends sitting and sharing the meal as we laughed together in a fun, free-spirited way. My ex had enjoyed socialising outside the home and hadn't cared much for quiet cosy evenings in, with close friends. One of the first things I went out to buy was a firepit and I organised for a pergola to be built. The garden was ready for a feast with friends!

Borrow from Jacqueline

Many years ago, when I was supporting one of my clients through her heartbreak recovery process, she told me the loveliest thing, which I have used in my toolkit ever since:

"Shelley, you told me to add some metaphorical colour into my home but I just really struggled with it. I've been feeling so uninspired. So I thought about one of my idols, Jacqueline Kennedy Onassis, and I asked myself: *what would Jacqueline do?* Jacqueline loved the vibrancy of blue cornflowers and planted them all over the tired gardens of the White House to make them beautiful again after many years of neglect, so I stuck up zingy pictures of cornflowers all over my bedroom wall. I borrowed from Jacqueline!"

If you're feeling like you're lacking in inspiration: borrow some from someone you admire!

Today you're going to ... add some vibrancy to your home

What can you do to add a touch of vibrancy to your home? How can you add a sense of 'you-ness' into your home – something that represents part of your vision for your life ahead?

Write out your idea and then do one small thing, right away, to make a move towards achieving that. (In my case, my first small move was to start researching pergolas that would fit into my garden.)

18.

Fuelling the fire, one day at a time

With a growth-oriented mindset of curiosity, a clear vision and the right environment, every day presents a new opportunity to actively choose the direction in which you're heading. In this step, we are going to fuel your success with the setting of one of the most important life skills I have ever learnt. This skill is at the heart of my personal growth philosophy and is embedded in all the teaching materials I create.

Daily intention setting helps you craft your life's vision

Your vision of the things you want in your future is a kind of North Star – a flickering light in the distance, guiding you forwards as you navigate through the adventures of the twists and turns of life.

Like any kind of fire, your vision needs a source of fuel. The flames need to be tended. The energy of the flames won't stay alive for long without continual care taken to keep the fire alive. That is why you should fuel your vision for yourself by setting an intention, every day.

Cultivating success

In my spring garden, I didn't just imagine what I wanted to create then walk away and hope that it would somehow magically grow in that way. Once I had envisioned exactly what I wanted to create, I started to cultivate this vision by sowing seeds, planting plants and tending to the garden on a daily basis. I nourished it with my time, loving attention and resources as I continually shaped it day after day.

Following the blueprint set by your vision, a *daily practice of intention setting* allows you to cultivate your miracle life little by little, day by day. It takes the pressure off you feeling that you have to have a 'perfect' plan for the year ahead and gets you away from the idea that you have to push yourself so hard, to achieve what you want.

A habit of intention setting

Our daily habits are one of the most fundamental parts of who we are. They shape our lives.

People who cultivate the habit of consciously defining the shape of the day ahead, give themselves an incredible edge in life and create fertile ground for their dreams to come true.

Habits are formed by repetition. If you can keep a practice up for 30 days straight, you will have started to form a habit. Give it a go!

Today you're going to ... start a habit of daily intention setting

Every day is a new opportunity to set an intention and to live in alignment with your vision in a mindful way. My life has been improved immensely by a daily practice that I've been doing for the last 10 years – waking up each morning and setting a clear intention for the day. I choose one important thing to focus on every morning (something that is in alignment with my values and vision) and then answer three simple questions:

- **What do I want to create or make happen today?**
- **Why do I want this?**
- **How will I do it?**

Here is my personal example from this morning:

This morning when I woke up my primary intention was: today I want to create an opportunity for a memorable moment of connection with my partner.

Why? Connection is one of my highest values. I want to do this because I have been very busy and distracted these last few days, and I think we would both benefit from reconnecting as it will make me feel happier.

How will I do this? I will do this by finishing work a little early, so we have a peaceful hour together before dinner.

I'd like you to complete this exercise tomorrow morning. When you wake up, complete your answers to the questions ...

- What do I want to create or make happen today?

- Why do I want this?

- How will I do it?

. . . .
. . . .
. . . .
. . . .
. . . .
. . . .
. . . .
. . . .
. . . .
. . . .
. . . .
. . . .
. . . .
. . . .
. . . .
. . . .
. . . .
. . . .
. . . .
. . . .
. . . .
. . . .
. . . .
. . . .
. . . .

129

19.

A warm welcome

As you start to cultivate your miracle life, you can amplify your successes through the very simple act of welcoming in positivity. In this next step, we're going to reinforce that positivity through the lens of appreciation.

A lifelong adventure

Building on your habit of daily intention setting, you will start to see that life is not about a single destination and big lofty goals - it's about seeing life as a continual, lifelong adventure and recognising the daily small 'wins' of honouring those intentions.

What tiny 'win' can you celebrate today? Here's one for you: you have just read another section of this book. That means you are continuing to support yourself, invest in your future and set yourself up for success. Please give yourself a massive metaphorical pat on the back for that, right now!

If you are able to celebrate small successes, you will find that your confidence starts to go up and momentum will build.

The gratitude habit

Over the last few years, gratitude has become a central theme in self-development circles. That's because it is the greatest of amplifiers.

The more we acknowledge a success and appreciate its value, the more we are training our brain to seek out the things that make our lives better.

Gratitude isn't just about reinforcing habits though – it is an emotive act of appreciation that is a core relationship skill. The more you appreciate something, the more you will see it appear in your life, because we always notice the things that we put our energy into.

Taking a closer look

When you appreciate your life, you are also developing the skill of appreciating yourself ... in all your wild, wonderful, natural, glorious beauty. Like all other relationship skills, self-appreciation is something that can be learnt and mastered over time, with practice and repetition. It is worth it ... because you are worth it! (Sorry l'Oréal for pinching your line, but it is a brilliant and apt statement that taps into something really important.)

The vital thing with gratitude and appreciation is that you don't just skim over the superficial surface. You need to lean in to look closely at the non-obvious things. Imagine the early days of falling in love with someone—the little details you notice about them and the quirky things that make them unlike anyone you have ever met before—and cast those same loving eyes over your own life. If you can stretch your senses and imagination into the details of your life that you can appreciate, you will find many treasures.

I end every day by writing out a list of all the things I am appreciative of. It's so simple, but it makes such a difference in my life. I ensure that I stretch my imagination by writing out a list of 20 things. That way I get beyond the most obvious ones and find my way into new and interesting territories ... and into the riches of my inner secret garden.

Today you're going to ... appreciate the small things

What do you appreciate in your life, right now? I'd like you to write out a list of 20 things you appreciate today. Within that list of 20 things, make sure you include at least three things that you appreciate about yourself. I am going to get you started with the first one.

I appreciate that ...

1. I have picked myself up and worked through another step towards thriving.

2. ....
....
....
....

3. ....
....
....
....

4. ....
....
....
....

5. ....
....
....
....

6. ....
....
....

7.

8.

9.

10.

11.

12.

13.

14.

15.

16.

17.

18.

19.

20.

20.

Basking and presence

If you dial the energy of appreciation up one notch, you can tip over from gratitude and appreciation into a full-bodied sense of presence.

Presence is an invitation to love

When you are present and connected to the sensations around you (rather than the scent-trail of the future or the echoes of the past), you are present to yourself and, from that sense of presence, you are able to share yourself with the world.

Being present—basking in the moment—is how you fully live your life.

By allowing joy and rapture to seep into the present moment, you are inviting love into your life – your love of the world, your love of yourself, your love of others.

Like attracts like and so, in that way, love will find you back.

Learn to bask in the moment

One summer's day, months into my heartbreak recovery journey, I was sitting in my garden with a hot cup of tea in my hands. The cup was a blue handmade earthenware cylinder with a slightly rough texture. I could feel the heat on my hands through its rough texture. The sun and a gentle breeze seemed to simultaneously kiss my face, in a moment of 'just right-ness'. I found myself breathing in the aromas of the heady jasmine combined with the mysterious scents of recently watered soil.

This moment of connection with all my senses made me realise that I was coming back to life again. That I was truly and fully present in the moment. I was basking!

Trauma dulls our senses to allow the body to focus on the life-critical cues in the environment. I'd entirely lost my sense of taste and smell for many months when I was consumed with grief and this was long before COVID appeared on the scene! (People talk a lot about losing their appetite in heartbreak – this loss of senses is one of the main reasons for that.)

Like any muscle you are developing, the muscle of presence is one that takes time to build. But it's worth investing in it, as it is your key to a life filled with love (including self-love, our starting point here), particularly when amplified with appreciative joy.

Today you're going to ... be fully present

Here is an exercise that I teach my clients that sounds simple but has profound consequences.

I'd like you to take your favourite drink—hot or cold—and take it outside. You might want to prepare a little flask or go to pick something up from your nearest cafe.

If you have a garden or a balcony or any private outdoor space of your own, that's a perfect place to go. Otherwise, a nearby park (or anywhere where you can feel a sense of nature around you) is suitable.

Find a lovely spot where you can stand or sit for a few moments.

- When you are in your spot, with your drink in your hand, I'd like you to take a moment to connect with all five of your senses.
- What can you feel on your skin (through the wind, the sun)? What temperature is your drink? How does the drink feel against your lips? How does your body feel right now? Are you warm or cool?
- Draw a deep breath in through your nose. What can you smell? What aromas can you pick up from the plants around you? Can you smell the earth? Does the earth smell dry or moist?
- What can you hear? Can you pick up any sounds from the plants or trees near you? Can you hear your own heart?
- How does your drink taste? Does it taste exactly the same as when you are inside or are there any nuances that make it taste different?

Allow your eyes to seek the most beautiful part of the nature around you. What are you looking at?

As you connect with your senses, allow yourself to feel uplifted by the beauty of the natural world. Allow yourself to feel connected to all of your senses and the pleasures they bring you.

21.

Play

Playfulness is the ultimate sense of connection, flow, self-expression, creativity, curiosity and presence—the ultimate in pleasure—all rolled into one!

When grief stops us in our tracks, there is no energy for play – everything becomes about survival and adjusting to the new 'normal'. Life can lose its magic and colour. In those times, even if you don't feel like it, it's important to go through the motions of doing something, to start to lay down new habits and create an energetic shift.

The light in you

I want you to let your light shine. The way you are going to start raising your brightness is to exercise a bit of playfulness. That means connecting with something you love and allowing yourself to get lost in the moment with it.

When my marriage ended, everything became so serious. Endless lawyers, heavy conversations, pain, tears, anguish ... it had gone on so long that I had forgotten how to have fun. I had to force myself to start enjoying life again by actively making time for fun. It might sound like an oxymoron but I *made* myself have fun.

I had always loved the idea of salsa dancing. As a child I used to dance endlessly—whirling round and round in circles and losing myself in the music—but it had been years since I had really let loose on any kind of dance floor. My ex hadn't been much of a dancer, and I'd always felt a little self-conscious dancing around him, so I had dampened that desire down. When we separated, I forced myself to take salsa classes and ... oh my! ... it really brought me back to life! I felt sensual, I felt playful, I felt silly at times and just didn't care. When I danced, I was in full flow!

I realised that having fun was part of putting my identity back together again and strengthening my boundaries and sense of self by tapping into knowing what I really enjoyed. I followed the breadcrumb trail of the things I really loved and, building on the success of my salsa dancing, I started doing more and more things that filled me with playful joy!

The more fun I had, the more I felt my radiance filling up my body again. People started to remark that I was looking much more 'myself'. I knew I was starting to come back.

Today you're going to ... get playful

What are the things you love doing that make you lose yourself in the moment?

If you can't think of anything then don't worry – that's not just normal, it is also almost expected after heartbreak. You might find that you need to dig deep into your past to mine out some abandoned longings of your heart. Think back to the last time you lost yourself in the joy of the moment – when time just slipped away unnoticed. What were you doing?

Start by writing out some ideas.

From those ideas, I'd like you to choose one 'play project' for yourself and take a firm action, right now, towards getting going as quickly as possible on doing something that you might enjoy.

It's important that you don't just *think* about doing it but that you take concrete actions to *actually do* it, as soon as possible. If you want to truly and fully recover from heartbreak and create a rich and magical future, you need to keep your commitments to yourself. (Remember: you set the standards for how you allow others to treat you and those standards start with how you treat yourself, so keeping your commitments to yourself is important!)

*Shift your perspective and
watch the world transform
around you.*

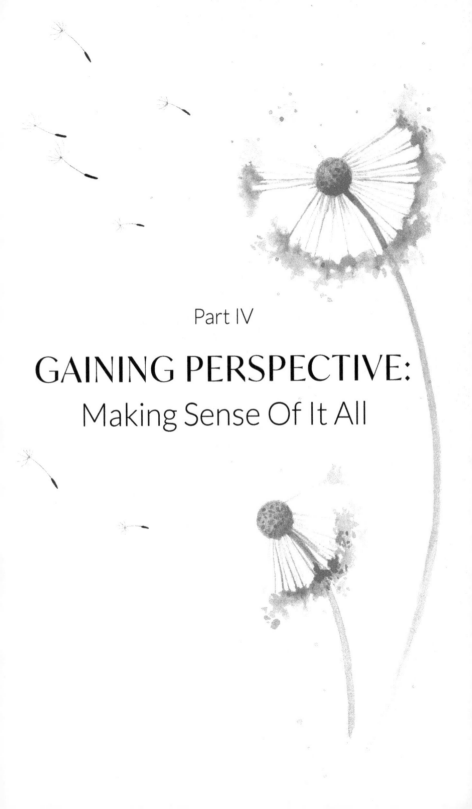

Part IV

GAINING PERSPECTIVE:
Making Sense Of It All

Hello, my lovely! How are you? Are you starting to feel the real YOU shining through yet? Even if you don't yet feel any sense of 'shine', do you feel a little bit of a sense of *hope* ... a little glimmer of light through the clouds?

About eight months after my heart shattered into pieces, I felt that my life was finally taking off again. As the days went by and my boundaries grew stronger and my sense of self slowly filled up inside me, I could feel that glimmer of light inside me growing ever brighter. I knew that I was changing. I felt a sense of power in me that I had never quite felt before ... but, at the same time, something still felt off-kilter.

In the past I probably would have brushed that feeling off. Until now I had been used to hiding my own feelings from myself but now my inner work had led me to listen carefully to that sense of anxiety that quietly kept on tugging at my sleeve. What was it? What was this feeling trying to tell me? What did I need?

I was quietly reflecting on those questions as I sat in my garden one afternoon. The air was rich with flowers in full bloom – the garden rewarding me for my efforts, yielding a sensual and heady mix of fragrances, sights and sounds. I watched a lazy bumble bee trace its way across the borders, from flower to flower, as it droned loudly. With legs heavy with pollen and a belly full of nectar it swerved its way towards me, paused in the air just in front of my nose, before proceeding to rise up and up above me. It made me smile. I felt like we'd shared a moment together – both drinking in the beauty of the garden before saying a brief hello to each other. My attention followed it upwards as I found myself imagining what it saw as it looked down.

I was surprised by what I 'saw'. I saw myself sitting in my chair in the harmony of my own green little sanctuary. I saw my comfort and my joy as I experienced the pleasures of the garden I had created. I saw the well-tended perimeter boundaries of the passionflower and clematis vines enclosing my space. And then ... I saw the world outside—the buzzy, busy wilderness beyond—and I realised that I was hiding. My sanctuary had become my limiting container. I realised that I had become afraid to leave it. I knew why I was afraid – how could I possibly open up to let the world in again? How could I ever take the risk of loving again?

That was the fourth and final major turning point in my healing journey. I realised that unless I pushed myself that little bit further, I was going to limit the possibility of what lay ahead of me. I knew that I needed a fuller perspective and at the same time that the same perspective needed to have me at its centre. I needed to rise above everything I had just been through and take a wider view, so I could fly free from any limitations that were holding me back.

I found a way of doing that work and it changed my life. In the pages ahead I'm going to take you through a perspective-finding series of steps that will open up many avenues of insight for you.

When I'm working face-to-face, coaching individuals through to the other side of their heartbreak, it's at this point in the journey that I start to see deep transformation happen. You may find this intimidating or you may find this exciting. Whatever you're feeling, keep going. All the work you're doing in this healing journey will be 'banked', like currency, inside you – it is all of profound value and it will all contribute to a richer, deeper, more meaningful life.

You will soon be flying.

22.

The perspective of your relationship with your ex

In the last section, we did some important work in clearing things out, making discerning choices and taking things out of the shadows. It is now time for us to start doing some deeper clearing, bringing things out of the metaphorical hidden 'cupboards' in your mind – it's time to shift to an internal spring clean so you can see through the clutter and gain profound insights into your relationship with yourself, your past and the people around you.

The core ingredients of a healthy relationship

When people talk about good relationships, they often get a little bit fixated on the concept of 'chemistry' (the alchemy of those warm, bubbly, fuzzy, liberating, butterfly-in-tummy, inspiring, uplifting feelings associated with the early days of meeting a new potential soulmate) but a healthy relationship involves far more than just chemistry. There are many more ingredients in the mix.

Relationships come in different flavours but in the course of my work I have found that there are some essential ingredients that must be in place, for a relationship to truly thrive. These core ingredients build, one on top of the other ...

1. Connection

Connection is made up of a beautiful mix of understanding ('I get you'), validation ('I hear what you're saying'), intimacy ('I feel emotionally close to you'), attunement ('I'm sensitive to your needs') and responsiveness ('I'll show you that I care'). For me, personally, connection is my absolute highest value – I thrive on connection.

2. Safety

In the cocoon of a safe relationship, you can be totally yourself. You can express feelings and needs, and you are able to ask directly for your needs to be met without fear of ridicule or recrimination. There is no harsh judgement when you are being your most powerful, vibrant self – nor when you are a vulnerable version of yourself.

3. Self-expression

A solid partnership allows the 'I' and the 'we' to coexist. Both partners' needs are important and the two do not become merged into an enmeshed codependent blur. This 'interdependence' is supported by good boundaries, mutual encouragement and support (in other words, the elements you would see in a good friendship ... and friendship is an important part of relationships).

4. Creativity

Creativity is a visionary form of growth. In the context of the self, it is about putting energy into the risk of expressing the unique vision that lies within. In the context of relationships, it is about mutual problem solving and working together in a solution-minded way, meeting challenges with fresh solutions, with a willingness to learn and embrace the challenges and work that naturally comes with all relationships. It is difficult to grow alongside someone who has no desire to learn and to grow but it is a wonderful experience to overcome obstacles and achieve new heights together.

5. Trust

Trust takes more than the *congruence* of words aligning with actions – it's about knowing that the other person is looking out for your needs and will factor these needs into their own decisions and choices. Trust is one of the most precious of all the relationship ingredients, as it takes time to build but can easily be broken in many ways, including in the form of manipulation (defined as someone sneaking in their own needs, cuckoo-like, under the guise of something supposedly being of benefit to you).

6. Adventure
A relationship can exist without a sense of adventure but, with this ingredient added into the mix with all the others, it will radiate good health. What I mean by 'adventure' is a sense of shared vision and the courage to take risks together. Setting off on any adventure requires the courage to be vulnerable as well as the strength to envision what lies ahead.

7. Presence
One of the most beautiful definitions of love I know is that of 'basking in each other' – where there is simply the pure pleasure of just being in each other's presence. Presence is often overlooked as a core relationship factor, perhaps because it is so uncomplicated that it is not deemed noteworthy, but it is a critical one for a partnership to thrive.

8. Receptivity
Acknowledging and affirming the support your partner gives you and recognising the ways in which they improve your quality of life will nourish and nurture a relationship. As we already know, appreciation and gratitude are the great amplifiers of positivity.

9. Play
Playfulness can be expressed in many ways, whether in the form of an easy interaction or as the intimate pleasures of the senses or in a lively spirit of fun. This ingredient is the purest form of love and essential for a high-quality relationship.

10. Acceptance

When you accept your partner, you don't try to manipulate them or change them. You love them exactly as they are. The same goes for the relationship with the self.

11. Integrity

When you have a relationship of integrity, you bring your whole self and are able to accept the wholeness of your partner. This goes beyond 'acceptance' to an ownership of the shadow selves – those trickier parts of ourselves that we relegate into darkness and try to disown. In the full light of love, the shadows become fully integrated.

12. Reflection

When we look at reflections, we can fully see ourselves. An enlightened relationship will allow you to see yourself, all the more clearly, and to take learnings from that reflection. The journey in this book has taken you to this point of reflection. We are now going to take a closer look through the lens of all the other relationship ingredients.

Taking stock of the remnants of the relationship

This is the moment that you will need to summon your inner resources of strength. It will be worth it because once you have worked through these heavy layers, what will follow will be unrestricted growth.

We're going to do an inventory of your relationship with your ex, through the lens of the 'core ingredients of a healthy relationship'. I imagine that this will not sound like a joyous step for you. You might have reached that place of serenity and feel that the last thing you want to do is to stir things up again.

It's like wading into a garden pond – it's going to look really mucky for a moment. If you don't wade in, though, you won't be able to pull those final weeds out. They will still be there, rooted in place, stealing precious oxygen and suffocating the other plants. I promise that with each step it will get easier and easier … until suddenly you will find that you are out in the fresh, oxygenated air of clarity. I will be with you every step of the way through this next cycle of growth.

It will be worth it – you'll soon see.

Today you're going to ... do an 'ex-inventory'

In the context of those crucial relationship ingredients, you're going to take stock of what was and wasn't present in your relationship.

Set yourself some time to do this. You might get it done quickly, you might decide to take longer, but most people find it takes at least an hour. There is no rush to finish. It may take time to fill in the details, but just keep going and keep filling in the details as they come to mind. Work at whatever pace suits you. The maximum I would recommend spending on it is a few hours – if you are spending more than that, recognise that you might be stuck in the 'denial' or 'bargaining' phases of grief, holding on tightly to the remnants of the relationship. Don't judge yourself if that's the case – just acknowledge it.

You are going to need a pen and several sheets of paper.

As you're writing your way through this exercise, avoid making too many judgements (either of yourself or of them). This is just an exercise in taking 'inventory'—in other words OBSERVATION—we are not trying to resolve everything right now.

Write your answers to the questions, in the shape of full sentences (rather than one-word answers).

1. **Connection**
    - Did you feel 'seen', 'heard' and 'understood'?
    - Were there times you ever felt lonely in the relationship?
    - Were they able to pick up what was going on for you or did you feel invisible to them?
    - Did they go out of their way to show you that they cared about your feelings?

2. **Safety**
    - Were there times you felt unsafe with them?
    - Did you ever feel dismissed, ridiculed or criticised?
    - When you were feeling your 'best self' how did they respond?
    - What about when you were feeling insecure, unwell or tired – were they supportive?

3. **Self-expression**
    - Did you feel like an equal partner in the relationship?
    - Did you feel that you lost your identity in any way, in the relationship?
    - Did you have clarity around the difference between their needs and yours?
    - Were you able to maintain healthy boundaries in the relationship?

4. **Creativity**
    - Were there any recurring issues or arguments or negative feelings that you just couldn't solve together?
    - Was there something you needed from them that they were unable to give you?
    - Did you feel comfortable asking for your needs to be met?
    - Did you collectively see relationship challenges as 'opportunities' to grow or 'obstacles' to happiness?

5. **Trust**
    *   Think back to those very early days. What were the early 'red flags'? (We define 'red flags' here as the warning signals that you may have intuitively felt that would have given you an indication that you weren't compatible or that something was awry, from the outset.)
    *   Did they ever do anything to break your trust?
    *   Were they ever unreliable?
    *   Did they ever lie to you or break a promise about something important?

6. **Adventure**
    *   Did you have a shared vision for your relationship (things you wanted to do and experience together)?
    *   Were you able to be vulnerable with them about your dreams and vision for your life?
    *   Did you feel energised to try new things with them?
    *   Did you talk about your own visions for your individual aspirations?

7. **Presence**
    *   Did they spend quality time with you?
    *   Did they enjoy being around you?
    *   Did you enjoy being around them?
    *   Did you ever long for things like time, attention or cuddles but were left wanting?

8. **Receptivity**
    *   Did you appreciate what they did for you?
    *   Did they appreciate what you did for them?
    *   Was it easy for you to receive love from them (in the form of gifts, time, kind words, acts of service, touch)?
    *   Were they receptive to your love for them?

9. **Play**
   - Were there things you loved doing together?
   - Did you have fun together?
   - Did you feel a blissful sense of abandonment with them – that sense of just being fully in the flow of the moment?
   - Was it a priority in the relationship for you to do pleasurable things together (rather than just being focused on practical things or day-to-day mundanities)?

10. **Acceptance**
    - Was there anything about them that made you incredibly unhappy?
    - What was it about them that made you happy?
    - Did you have any value clashes?
    - What did they like about you?

11. **Integrity**
    - What were the positive things about this relationship (e.g. they introduced you to a different genre of music, you travelled to destinations you'd never been before etc.)
    - What six positive traits and qualities did you like, admire and respect about them the most?
    - Was there anything about them that made you put them on a pedestal and that you overly admired in them?
    - Was there anything about them you just couldn't stand to be around?

12. **Reflection**
    - What did you learn about yourself from the relationship?
    - What did you learn about what you need from a relationship?
    - What did you learn about love from the relationship?
    - What did you learn about life from the relationship?

23.

The perspective of the past

In the last exercise we zoomed upwards, like the bumble bee in my garden. We looked down at your relationship with your ex and made a few observations. It's now time for us to hover even higher and take in the perspective of your earlier relationships.

A pause for another quick check in

How are you feeling?

Ask yourself that question and notice all the feelings that rise to the surface.

If you did a deep declutter of your living space, did you find that there was a moment when you felt totally overwhelmed and exhausted? That often happens at the moment when you've taken everything out of the cupboards and you have what looks like a huge mess in front of you. It can feel overwhelming. You might have needed to dig deep and summon some energy reserves to start putting things back in order again. Once things started to get back in order, once you'd weeded out the clutter of what you didn't want to take forward into your future, you are likely to have suddenly felt a fresh rush of energy rise again. That same point will be on the horizon again for you soon ... but we have a bit more clearing out to do first.

Remember: if you are feeling overwhelmed at any point, you can take a look back at the exercise in Step 9 'When it all feels too much'. If you're feeling exhausted, acknowledge that to yourself ... and then carry on when you're ready.

Like all of the 28 steps, make sure you don't skip this one. All of these exercises will soon start to make sense and, from the sequence we are working through, you will be able to start to weave the threads together.

Our early lives set our relationship blueprints

In our early years, we learn how to interact with others. We carry those relationship habits through into our adult lives without even knowing they are there. These patterns are the invisible threads that set the tone for all of our future relationships and the blueprint for our expectations. When we shine a light on these patterns and make them visible, we can start to make choices about whether we want to carry on with the same kinds of interactions or whether we want to find new ways of doing things.

Today you're going to ... do a 'relationship-inventory'

You're now going to repeat the previous exercise but this time you're going to do it for the three most 'significant' relationships in your life. Within this list I'd like you to include:

- Your primary caregiver when you were growing up (for example, your mother or father)
- A significant friendship
- Your most important previous romantic relationship (if you have previously had one or, if you didn't, another significant relationship with either a friend or a family member)

Take out your pen and sheets of paper again and answer all the same questions you answered in the 'Checking in on the foundations of the relationship' exercise, for each of those three people, writing their name at the top of the sheets. Again, do take your time, but don't let this run on too long – it's still just an inventory exercise of observation.

As a reminder, here are the questions:

1. **Connection**
- Did you feel 'seen', 'heard' and 'understood'?
- Were there times you ever felt lonely in the relationship?
- Were they able to pick up what was going on for you or did you feel invisible to them?
- Did they go out of their way to show you that they cared about your feelings?

2. **Safety**
- Were there times you felt unsafe with them?
- Did you ever feel dismissed, ridiculed or criticised?

- When you were feeling your 'best self' how did they respond?
- What about when you were feeling insecure, unwell or tired – were they supportive?

3. Self-expression
- Did you feel like an equal partner in the relationship?
- Did you feel that you lost your identity in any way, in the relationship?
- Did you have clarity around the difference between their needs and yours?
- Were you able to maintain healthy boundaries in the relationship?

4. Creativity
- Were there any recurring issues or arguments or negative feelings that you just couldn't solve together?
- Was there something you needed from them that they were unable to give you?
- Did you feel comfortable asking for your needs to be met?
- Did you collectively see relationship challenges as 'opportunities' to grow or 'obstacles' to happiness?

5. Trust
- Think back to those very early days. What were the early 'red flags'? (We define 'red flags' here as the warning signals that you may have intuitively felt that would have given you an indication that you weren't compatible or that something was awry, from the outset.)
- Did they ever do anything to break your trust?
- Were they ever unreliable?
- Did they ever lie to you or break a promise about something important?

6. **Adventure**
- Did you have a shared vision for your relationship (things you wanted to do and experience together)?
- Were you able to be vulnerable with them about your dreams and vision for your life?
- Did you feel energised to try new things with them?
- Did you talk about your own visions for your individual aspirations?

7. **Presence**
- Did they spend time with you?
- Did they enjoy being around you?
- Did you enjoy being around them?
- Did you ever long for things like time, attention or cuddles but were left wanting?

8. **Receptivity**
- Did you appreciate what they did for you?
- Did they appreciate what you did for them?
- Was it easy for you to receive love from them (in the form of gifts, time, kind words, acts of service, touch)?
- Were they receptive to your love for them?

9. **Play**
- Were there things you loved doing together?
- Did you have fun together?
- Did you feel a blissful sense of abandonment with them – that sense of just being fully in the flow of the moment?
- Was it a priority in the relationship for you to do pleasurable things together (rather than just being focused on practical things or day-to-day mundanities)?

10. Acceptance

- Was there anything about them that made you incredibly unhappy?
- What was it about them that made you happy?
- Did you have any value clashes?
- What did they like about you?

11. Integrity

- What were the positive things about this relationship (e.g. they introduced you to a different genre of music, you travelled to destinations you'd never been before etc.)
- What six positive traits and qualities did you like, admire and respect about them the most?
- Was there anything about them that made you put them on a pedestal and that you overly admired in them?
- Was there anything about them you just couldn't stand to be around?

12. Reflection

- What did you learn about yourself from the relationship?
- What did you learn about what you need from a relationship?
- What did you learn about love from the relationship?
- What did you learn about life from the relationship?

24.

The perspective of your relationship with you

One more round of an inventory and then we will be done with this! Bear with me – you're nearly there!

This work might make you feel momentarily disoriented, but once you have completed this sequence, you will see that things will start to feel much, much better. Lean in and do the work and you will reap big rewards.

Today you're going to ... do a 'self-inventory'

This exercise that you're now going to do is to repeat the 'Checking in on the foundations of the relationship' exercise, but this time you are going to be answering all of the questions about the way you have looked after yourself.

To save you from having to do any kind of mental gymnastics to answer the questions, I have rephrased them all for you here (and omitted some of the previous questions that aren't as pertinent). So please go ahead and answer the following questions as honestly as you can, with no sense of judgement or shame.

Write your answers to the questions, in the shape of full sentences (rather than one-word answers).

1. Connection
- Do you feel connected to your feelings?
- Are there times you ever feel lonely?
- Do you ever tune out or dissociate from your feelings?
- Do you ever take time to explore your needs and why you might be feeling a certain way?

2. Safety
- Have you ever deliberately caused yourself pain in any way (physically or emotionally)?
- Do you ever dismiss, ridicule or criticise your own feelings?
- Do you ever allow yourself to shine (expressing your successes) or do you prefer to stay hidden?
- Are you kind to yourself when you're feeling insecure, unwell or tired?

3. Self-expression
- Do you look after your needs?
- Do you feel a strong sense of self?
- Are you in tune with your needs?
- Do you have good inner boundaries?

4. Creativity
- Are you good at finding creative solutions to support your dreams?
- Do you stand by your dreams and make time for them?
- Are you good at finding ways to get your needs met?
- Do you see challenges as 'opportunities' to grow or 'obstacles' to happiness?

5. **Trust**
- Are you a trustworthy person?
- Have you ever let yourself down?
- Are you ever unreliable?
- Do you ever lie or break important promises to yourself?

6. **Adventure**
- Do you have a vision for things you'd like to do in life?
- Are you able to take risks, to achieve your dreams?
- Do you feel energised trying new things?
- Do you have aspirations you'd love to achieve?

7. **Presence**
- Do you prioritise time for yourself when you need it?
- Do you enjoy being in your own company?
- Do you enjoy spending time with other people?
- Do you take time for self-care?

8. **Receptivity**
- Are you able to appreciate your own life?
- Are there things you are grateful for?
- Can you acknowledge your own gifts and talents?
- Do you love yourself?

9. **Play**
- Are there things you love doing?
- Do you make time for having fun?
- Do you ever feel fully in the flow of the moment?
- Do you make time for the things you love doing?

10. Acceptance

- Does your life make you incredibly happy?
- What makes you most happy?
- Is there anything that is important for you in your life that you never make time for?
- What do you like about yourself?

11. Integrity

- What things would you love to have in your life that you don't yet have?
- What six positive traits and qualities would you most like to have?
- What qualities from others would you like to integrate into your own identity?
- What parts of your life or your sense of self might you be rejecting?

12. Reflection

- What have you learnt about yourself recently?
- What have you learnt about your needs recently?
- What have you learnt about love recently?
- What have you learnt about life recently?

25.

Weaving all the threads together

Now that you've got a lot of relationship information out of the metaphorical 'cupboards' of the recesses of your mind with these three types of inventories (with your ex, your most significant relationship and with yourself) we're going to do some sorting and sifting. We are going to weave together the learnings and put things into their rightful places.

Remember back in Step 10 when we packed up the remnants of your ex's things into boxes marked 'Give Back', 'Let Go' and 'Treasure'? Well, we're just about to do almost the same thing with this emotional clutter ... we're going to sift through and sort things into their rightful boxes.

Sifting through to find the *real* treasure

I realised I was fully over my ex when I no longer felt any anger towards him. It wasn't that I completely overlooked some of his very hurtful behaviour – it was just that I didn't *care* about it any more. The energetic charge was completely gone. It was around this time that I found that I was able to look back at the relationship and see some of the positive benefits it had brought me. The positive things I'm talking about here aren't the 'good memory' kind of benefits – what I am talking about is the deep understanding of the patterns of the past.

The real treasure of this terrible pain was that I was so steadfastly sure that I never EVER wanted to go through that again that it forced me to look deep inside myself and take full accountability, to identify the patterns that had led me there in the first place so that I could overcome those patterns and let my real inner self shine through.

Rather than just putting the pieces back together and hastily pasting over the cracks of the rupture, I took an honest look at the fault lines that had created the rupture in the first place. That was the real treasure: identifying what was mine, then sifting through to find the weeds amidst the plants.

Putting it all together

When you did the inventory exercises, you might have started to notice that there were common threads in the behaviours, feelings, traits, benefits and issues in all or many of these relationships. These are the threads that show you what didn't belong exclusively to the relationship but that belong to you and your life as a general pattern. They are part of the makeup of who you currently are and who you have been.

Amidst the common threads will be obvious treasures. Those are the positive things you want to acknowledge and carry forward into your future. That includes everything that you did in any of your relationships that you were really proud of and anything that you'd like more of in your life.

Within these common threads you will also find the less obvious treasures. These are the things you want to explore and perhaps weed out in the future.

Anything negative that doesn't fit into a common thread, doesn't 'belong' in your future and can go straight into the same 'Give Back' box that you created for your ex's physical clutter as you weeded his things out of your home – there's nothing for you there.

In this next exercise, you are going to identify what goes onto each of the three lists. To get you a little bit inspired, I will share the lists I wrote out after my divorce.

The positive common threads that I want more of in my life are:
- I'd like more fun and laughter in my life.
- I am at my happiest when I feel deeply connected to people I love.
- I want more people around me who share my values of healthy living, growth and development.

The common threads I would like to weed out in the future are:
- I've had a lot of emotionally unavailable people in my life. I'd like to work out why and what I need to do about it.
- My ex's behaviour echoes that of my mother's and of my first boyfriend. I'd like to know why.
- People in my life have often been untrustworthy. I'd like to work out how to stop that from happening.

The threads that 'belong' to my ex, which I am happy to see the back of now are:
- I will never again have to lie awake late at night, worrying about what he is doing and with whom.
- I won't have to feel that my needs aren't a priority anymore.
- I will no longer need to be concerned about his ever-fluctuating emotional states.

Today you're going to ... decide what goes where:

I'd like you to complete each of the three statements below:

1. **The positive common threads that I want more of in my life are:** (These items should be the qualities, themes and traits you admire and love in yourself and others.)

    . . . .

    . . . .

    . . . .

    . . . .

    . . . .

    . . . .

2. **The common threads I would like to weed out in the future are:** (Here are some additional prompts that might help you get started with this one:
    - One negative pattern I see consistently in my relationships is ...
    - What I am sorry for is ...
    - An ongoing pattern that started for me with my caregivers is ...
    - What I want to learn to avoid in the future is ...
    - What I don't understand about my relationships that I would like to learn more about is ...)

    . . . .

    . . . .

    . . . .

    . . . .

    . . . .

    . . . .

3. **The threads that 'belong' to my ex, which I am happy to see the back of now are:** (When you complete this statement, see if you can find things that weren't already on your '25 benefits of not being with your ex' exercise, from Step 2.)

. . . .
. . . .
. . . .
. . . .
. . . .
. . . .
. . . .
. . . .
. . . .
. . . .
. . . .
. . . .
. . . .
. . . .
. . . .
. . . .
. . . .
. . . .
. . . .
. . . .
. . . .
. . . .
. . . .

26.

Closing the chapter

In the last few steps, you completed a far-reaching inventory that will have given you great insight into the landscape of your relationships, as well as helpful insights around future areas to explore and develop. Well done! You've just done a huge piece of work.

You have reached an important juncture. This exercise will be your last moment of looking back, before you turn your head fully away from the past and start to look upwards and outwards, at the horizon ahead.

Defining the ending

Life is a constant series of endings and beginnings. Seasons come and go, people come in and out of your life, new chapters start and end. Even during the course of a day, we are in a state of constant transition, punctuated by our daily habits and practices (including getting up out of bed, starting breakfast, finishing breakfast, getting started on the day ... you get the picture!)

Right at the beginning of this journey, back in Step 1, we talked about 'disenfranchised grief'. Whilst cultures often put a lot of focus on celebrating the important 'beginnings' (such as a new job, an engagement, the birth of a baby, moving into a new home and so on) endings often go overlooked ... particularly those that relate to the end of a relationship (in the shape of breakups/ divorces/ separations). In the course of my many years as a relationship coach, I came to the realisation of how important it was for individuals going through a breakup to 'define' and honour a clear moment in time: the moment that represents the fact that the relationship has officially ended. The end of an era. It is time to come full circle and to close this gap.

The end of the story

It's quite normal, after a breakup, for people to ask you 'what happened?'

That happened to me endlessly, after my divorce.

There are two things to bear in mind with your response. The first consideration is boundaries: remember that you don't *have* to give people an assessment of your interior world ... it is totally up to you what you choose to share. We are all multifaceted human beings with a unique history and a unique set of needs, experiences, wishes, compatibilities, traits, emotions ... which are not easy to 'bottom line' without exploring the inner workings of our soul.

The second—and more important—consideration is that retelling the 'story' can often be a painful way of getting pulled back into the grieving process. After you have finished the process in this book, as you fully heal, you are going to want to move beyond your grief and you are not going to want to keep the story of your past relationship alive by rehashing it over and over again with the people around you.

My recommendation is that you maintain a boundary and, in your answer, that you help yourself to close the chapter by keeping your answer to a succinct one-sentence 'closed statement' (rather than an open-ended invitation to collectively discuss the subject). Here are some suggested one-line scripts for you below, which you can use if any of them resonate for you:

- I realised I was looking for something different in life.
- I discovered that we had different values.
- I chose a different pathway.

You will notice that all of these statements are framed from the perspective of the first-person individual 'I', rather than the implied partnership of 'we'. That framework allows you to take an empowered accountability for your story.

Are you ready to close the chapter?

To honour this ending and fully close this chapter, you're now going to write an important letter.

This will be your moment of full closure.

Today you're going to ... write a letter to close the chapter

For this exercise, you are going to write out a full letter to your ex, filling in the blanks below.

Find a comfortable place to sit and get yourself feeling nice and settled. Choose a time when you will not be disturbed, and you do not have any arrangements afterwards. You may want to light a candle.

All of the work you did in the inventory section of this chapter will help you to fill in the blanks and write clear and specific details. Say anything and everything you wish to say in this letter – don't hold anything back. Feel free to write in whatever format works for you and in any style that suits you, choosing language and words that resonate. You can add in additional sections if you'd like to do that and include whatever things you would like to say, but make sure that it is honest. Don't leave any of the sections out though – they are all important.

When you have finished writing this letter you will sign it, but you are NOT GOING TO SEND IT. Remember: this is all for *you* and *your* benefit. Instead, you are going to tear this letter into pieces and, if you have a candle, burn the pieces to symbolically release and let go. And then blow the candle out.

Dear ...

I am writing this letter today because I wish to say goodbye to you.

What I have admired, appreciated, valued, loved in you was ...

. . . .
. . . .
. . . .

The issues in the relationship that I would have liked to have been different were ...

. . . .
. . . .
. . . .

What I take responsibility for and what I am sorry for is ...

. . . .
. . . .
. . . .

What I forgive you for is ...

. . . .
. . . .
. . . .

What I wish for you in the future is ...

. . . .
. . . .

<Sign off with your name here>

27.

Writing your own story

Welcome to your fresh start! In this penultimate step we are going to reset your point of gravity.

The home inside you

I love this metaphor: if you look to others to create your miracle life, you are, effectively, *building your home inside someone else*. If, instead, you first find all of your resources inside you, you will be able to tune into your true values and build the foundations of your vision from a place of true integrity, following your own curiosity on your own adventures. That is where you find your pot of gold – on the other side of the rainbow is the home inside you.

Everything starts with a beautiful, healthy relationship with yourself. THAT is what will draw in your real-life partner – from that magnetic pull, emanating from your richly overflowing self-love and fully lived life.

Your relationship with yourself sets the tone for how others treat you and sets the standards for your life. Becoming your own supportive best friend and your own loving supportive partner will mean you will never again settle for anything less than the wonderfulness you truly deserve.

When you are able to trust yourself, you will be able to take the risk to trust others again. Love means taking a risk. And, believe me, it is worth it.

The 'real' love story

Romantic love is an incredibly powerful force. I respect it, I revere it and have endless time for it. And yet ... I have to share with you the most profound of all my learnings, from all my pain, all my joy and all my adventures ... Aunt Vonnie was right – the biggest love story of all is the one that we have with ourselves.

The hero's journey that you are going through is all bringing you closer to you. And that, my lovely, is the key to everything. When you are not just comfortable in your own skin, but are radiant within your own being, your life transforms. You are not here to reflect the glory of others. You are here to shine.

Writing your own story

When I emerged from my heartbreak, phoenix-like, people told me they had never seen me looking so powerfully radiant.

"Everything happens for a reason," they said, as their way of making sense of the pain I had been through. "Yes," I would reply. "That reason is whatever I decide it to be." Personally I never agree with the sentiment that everything happens for a reason. Neither would I say this to anyone.

I am the author of my story. I am not a passive character in a big cosmic fairytale. I am the maker of my own magic – the creator of my own journey.

Write it, rewrite it, review it, write it again...

Creating your own adventure is not a fixed, single-note exercise that you do once in your life. Your journey will take its twists and turns. As you strengthen your skills of self-love and self-awareness you will feel more and more comfortable with the idea of continually adapting, along the way.

Remember: this book contains a helicopter view on a foundation course of healing – you can circle back to repeat and deepen the work at any time. Many of my clients have reaped wonderful rewards from repeating the steps when they are further along in their healing journey. It's your journey – own it ... and enjoy it!

Today you're going to ... start your story

This is a letter you're going to be writing to yourself. It might feel a bit awkward at first, but it is worth doing, as it not only sets the foundations for your next stage of growth, but is also your first step towards true, happy independence and healthier relationships.

All of the work you have been doing in this chapter so far should help you in writing some of the detail in the letter.

After you've finished, you're going to do a symbolic gesture: Store the letter in a safe place. Set a reminder in your calendar for one year from now, when you will take it out and reread it. The purpose of doing this is to remind yourself of how far you have come.

This is the beginning of my next chapter. I am writing this today because I wish to set the stage for a brighter, happier future. A future filled with ...

. . . .
. . . .
. . . .

When it comes to relationships, what I am proud of myself for is ...

. . . .
. . . .
. . . .

The things I am going to focus on learning about are ...

. . . .
. . . .
. . . .

What I forgive myself for is ...

. . . .
. . . .
. . . .

What I wish for myself in the future is ...

. . . .
. . . .
. . . .

<Sign off with your name here>

28.

Throwing the doors open

Out of the embers, your phoenix heart rises.

It's time, my lovely. It's the moment to open the door to the most beautiful of adventures.

As your relationship with yourself grows ever stronger, day by day, you will find that you can fall and rise and fall and rise and fall and rise. You can take the risk because you can trust yourself and know that you have it in you to always rise again.

Once you can appreciate the beauty of the home you have inside you and you can take great pleasure in being inside your own skin, you are ready to let the world in again.

You are sowing the seeds of your enchanted future. You are tending to the garden of your soul and you know how to spot the weeds. What you do next is up to you – beautiful, vibrant, powerful you.

Look up, look ahead, look out. Say 'yes' to the adventures ahead, embrace risk, allow yourself to fall over and to pick yourself back up again, up again. There's a big, beautiful world out there – calling you out, calling you ahead.

There's light ahead – that light is you!

Today you're going to ... take the reins

Complete the following sentence:

My next courageous step towards my future is ...

. . . .
. . . .
. . . .
. . . .
. . . .
. . . .
. . . .
. . . .
. . . .
. . . .
. . . .
. . . .
. . . .
. . . .
. . . .
. . . .
. . . .
. . . .
. . . .
. . . .
. . . .
. . . .

You've got this.

Love,

Shelley

Biography

Shelley J Whitehead, an award-winning relationship coach with a unique blend of personal and professional experience, offers deep insights into the realms of love, loss, and personal growth. Born in South Africa and now London-based, her approach to coaching embodies resilience and wisdom with deep and soulful insight.

Shelley's own heart has walked through the fires of loss – from the heart-wrenching departure of a partner to cancer to the sudden dissolution of a marriage. From these ashes, she's unearthed a profound truth: heartbreak, in its rawest form, offers a mirror to the soul, illuminating hidden dreams and passions. With lyrical wisdom, Shelley guides individuals on a transformative journey through their heartbreak and steers them towards a life abundant in love and connection.

Over her decades in practice, Shelley has amassed a diverse set of qualifications and accreditations. Notably, she is a Certified Life Coach (New Insights UK, ACCPH), Certified Transpersonal Coach (IACTM), and Encounter-Centered Couples Coach (EcCT). Shelley also holds certifications in Ericksonian Hypnotherapy, Neuro-Linguistic Programming, and as an Advanced Authentic Self Empowerment Facilitator (ASE). She is accredited with the International Association of Coaches, Therapists, and Mentors (IACTM).

About the book

Healing Your Heartbreak takes you on a transformative journey out of the depths of heartbreak and into the vibrant sunshine of a renewed sense of self. Award-winning relationship coach Shelley J Whitehead's proven and meticulously crafted steps weave profound insights with practical exercises.

As an inspiring and soul-nurturing guide, the pages resonate with the wisdom and comforting spirit of an understanding best friend – one who feels your pain but can light the path to healing. With Shelley by your side, the scars of heartbreak will begin to mend with each step you take. Your relationship skills will begin to flourish and you will be able to open your heart to love again.

Designed as a 28-day odyssey, the steps can be taken consecutively in a single sprint or at whatever pace feels right for you. The key is the sense of continual progress – taking your time to put one foot in front of the other. As you traverse this sacred journey, you'll be equipped with newfound wisdom and a powerful sense of aliveness. You'll find yourself not merely healing but thriving.

A poetic tapestry of soulful guidance, this book promises not just recovery but a magically beautiful metamorphosis.

9 781982 287801